ESTRELLAS EN EL FUEGO (Stars In The Fire):
   The Alternative New Year's Day Spoken Word / Performance
   Extravaganza - 2014 Anthology

- First Edition.
- Volume I in a series.
- 160 pages.
- Trade Paperback.
- American contemporary poetry anthology.

*Commemorating the 20th Anniversary of The Alternative New Year's Day Spoken Word / Performance Extravaganza which takes place every January 1st in New York City.

Contact Information / Order Online:
http://www.spokenwordextravaganza.org/

Design and Layout by C. D. Johnson
Publishers: C. D. Johnson, Miriam Stanley, and Bruce Weber
Front Cover / Frontispiece entitled: "Star In The Fire"

ISBN: 0-9840982-9-1
ISBN 13: 978-0-9840982-9-3

Published by Rogue Scholars Press
New York, NY - USA

ESTRELLAS EN EL FUEGO

(Stars In The Fire)

**The Alternative
New Year's Day
Spoken Word / Performance
Extravaganza**

2014 Anthology

A.N.Y.D.S.W.P.E. Imprint

r

CONTENTS

CONTENTS Continued

CONTENTS Continued

INTRODUCTION

Welcome to this anthology celebrating the 20th anniversary of the Alternative New Year's Day Spoken Word / Performance Extravaganza.

It's unbelievable that an event that started out with a whisper and a prayer has been up and running for going on two decades.

This is the first anthology that we have undertaken, although during the very early years we asked participants to bring multiple copies of a piece of writing for a collating effort, and a special issue of Stained Sheets (a broadside I used to edit under the auspices of ABC NO RIO) featured very short poems by writers responding to the theme of our third year which was El Niño.

We wish we could have given all the writers / performers featured in the 2014 event a chance to appear in print but our early submission deadline precluded that from happening; in the natural and normal course of events some people were invited to perform after the deadline.

The Alternative (as we call it for short) started on January 1st, 1995 at Café Nico on Avenue A between East 6th and 7th Streets in the East Village (above the legendary Pyramid Club).

Larry Jones was the proprietor of the club and opened its doors to us for five fabulous years of high energy and raucous celebrations of the spoken word, performance, music, and dance.

One prize memory — lining the steps up to Nico with absconded copies of The Village Voice (which failed to even list our event) so that attendees could deservedly trample them.

From there we moved for two years to the now late lamented CBGB'S and then for two years to the Knitting Factory on Leonard Street in Tribecca (the first year in the wake of 911), and then for nine years to our longtime home at the Bowery Poetry Club (a big thank you to Bob Holman), last year to Dixon Place (thank you Ellie Covan), and now a new era dawning as we celebrate our anniversary at the great Nuyorican Poets Café (thank you Daniel Gallant and Jason Quinones).

There have been many wrinkles thrown in as the years have gone by — this year the anthology and last as well as this the incorporation of images drawn from the work of artists who participate in the ambitious holiday show at Richie Timperio's Sideshow Gallery on Bedford Avenue in Williamsburg.

- Bruce Weber

ACKNOWLEDGMENTS

There are so many people to thank for helping make the Alternative such a rewarding and successful experience each year. For our early years I am most indebted to Larry Jones for his support and collaboration. My wife Joanne Pagano Weber was instrumental for many years in terms of the set design and visual imagery surrounding the show. For the tenth year, she collaborated with Yuko Otomo on a radiant design that still sparkles in memory. Su Polo has created memorable sets for many, many years, bringing whimsy and creativity and unexpected materials into play. Miriam Stanley has served as associate producer for several years, and has also stepped up when other responsibilities or duties have pulled my attention away (including much of the early stages of this year's event).

Bob Heman designed our visuals for a number of years, and C. D. Johnson has been our graphic designer, web-maven, and now co-publisher (with Miriam and myself) of this anthology. C. D. has worked with our multifarious themes to seamlessly create an image, look and identity for past number of seasons. Our current staff, some of whom have helped for a number of events, includes Madeline Artenberg, Robert Roth, Ellen Aug Lytle, Boni Joi, Peter Kozlowski, Su Polo and Puma Perl, who help with the ins and outs and asides that make up putting this complex event together with its reach towards enlisting charitable donations such as food and books and the one year we collected coats.

The list of people who have helped make this event possible over the years is a long one and I am afraid I will miss mentioning key people, but let me give it a try: Grace Period, Jan McLaughlin, Brian Boyles, Tsaurah Litzky, Nigia Stephens, John Holt, Bob Hart, Nelson Alxndre, Cenen, Steve Dalachinsky, George Spencer, Peter Kernz, J. M. Thiesen de Gonzalez, Ice, Big Mike, Pete Dolack, Fran Luck, Jeanne Dickey, Tom O., Ngoma, David Huberman, Mindy Levokove, Susan Sherman, Alam and all our friends at the New York Copy Center, Books Through Bars, Regie Cabico, Steve Cannon, Rosette Capotorto, Pablo Felix, William Hohauser, Eleanor Levine, Material for the Arts, Amy Ooizinian, Pogo, Yarrow Reagen, Jackie Sheeler, Danny Shot and Lydia Tomkie, and our dear and muchly missed friends and staff, Jushi and Brant Lyon, and all the hosts and curators of New Year's days pasts, all of whom have helped so much to make each January 1st a remarkable day.

We'd also like the thank the audience, and specifically the East and West Village community that continues to show up every year, making the Alternative New Year's Day Spoken Word / Performance Extravaganza one of the most successful yearly poetry events to ever take place in New York City.

Finally, I want to again thank my wife Joanne Pagano Weber, who has attended every event and run the book and sales table and been there as a remarkable partner in every aspect of what we do.

- Bruce Weber

ESTRELLAS EN EL FUEGO

Twenty years and we are still
burning,
burning words,
sounds,
noise,
bringing our spirits to the stage…

We are all stars,
we will not be incinerated nor
eclipsed,
our voices in transit as we burn…
we burn…
we burn…

Come Celebrate 20 Years in
the Light! Through the storms,
through the fires, through the re-
cession, despite the developers
raising the rents and ousting peo-
ple – the Alternative New Year's
Day Extravaganza continues! This
annual event has become a tradi-
tion that gives voice to a culturally
diverse group of performers of all
ages. It is a multi-media event and
includes musicians and artists of
all kinds, in addition to the ram-
bunctious, irreverent poets who
have gathered together for the last
two decades. Join us at the leg-
endary Nuyorican Poets Café! Add
your poetic language to the mix!

- Miriam Stanley
- Puma Perl

Amber

Peach

September 2002

A peach is not a beech
If a peach was beached one would say,
"Why where did you come from?"
One must reach for the peach
And teach about the peach
But let's not preach about the peach
Nice to greet-cha and meet-cha, Machu Picchy
But I'm gonna eat-cha
A ripe peach is delectable, and sweet and juicy
A peach's juice drools down your chin
A peach titillates your taste buds

A peach slides down your throat
A peach pleasurably entices your nose
An intriguing, caressable, tactilely fuzzy skin
Free stone or cling-stone, yellow or white
A peach of a smile, a Georgia delight
You're a peach of a person, peachy-keen
Imbibe your peach brandy with pieces of brandied peach
Peace is not a beech
If peace was beached one would say,
"The covenant has been breached".
One must reach for peace
And teach about peace
But let's not preach about peace
Nice to please 'ya and tease 'ya, tower of peace-a
I'm gonna feast on 'ya
Peace is delectable and sweet and juicy
Peace titillates your taste buds
Peace slides down your throat
Peace pleasurably entices your nose
Peace is intriguing, caressable, tactilely velvet

Peace is free and organized, rainbow or bowed-rain
Peace brings you a smile, engages your brain
Transjetting from Georgia to Georgia
You're a peaceful kind of person
Smoke your peace pipe
Toast the continuing process of peace
The absence of war does not create a peach

———

Bio: *(Amber)* Amber is the cornucopia fruit and vegetable poet, apple to mushroom, orange to zucchini. Published in And Then, Chez Chez, and translated into Spanish in Venezuala. She has held monthly poetry events in her office for one and a half years. Amber : a fossilized resin from antediluvian plants.

Maria Aponte

A Question

A man asked me the other day, "What are you?"I said, "I beg your
pardon?" Seeing that he placed himself in an awkward position
he rephrased the question, "What is your nationality?" "I'm Puerto
Rican." He looked surprised. "But you don't look Puerto Rican, you
look Black!" *Boricua, Boriqueña,* Puerto Rican. Palm trees, soft
blue skies, water blue and deep. I am a mixture of spices grown in
warm, rich climates. I am the smell of tropical flowers that grow in
lush green hills. I am Indian. I am African. I am Spaniard. *Boriquen* a
green island of
sweet vegetation
sugar cane
rain forest
mountain roads
unwinding into essence. Mambo
Boleros
Décimas.

I am a good plate of
Mofongo
Pernil
I am a good drink of
Coquito
Cuba Libre!
I am pottery, poetry, and the art of my people, wrapped inside a
capsule transported through space. I can go backwards in time to our
Taino roots, to the paradise before Columbus. Or, I can forward to a
century of cement, brick, glass, confused society, work that pays less
than your rent, subway trains that don't work, rush hours, holidays,
where everything's "buy, buy," American Style.
Yes, I am all these things.
What are you?

(*From "Transitions Of A Nuyorican Cinderella", 2012)

3

Maria Arrillaga

Ozymandias

To José Ferrer

After viewing "Cyrano," the movie, I went to sleep
I ran into him in my dreams
Not with the elongated ugly nose that earned him the coveted
"Oscar"
But with the beauty of a man totally dressed in white
Freshly shaven, neat, fashionable haircut
Perfectly groomed
He wore
A suit, shirt and tie, shoes and socks
Everything pure white
Around him one could sense the aura of deserving men
From the perception of my recall in chance meetings
Such as when JFK passed near me at the San Juan Airport and left
me numb with his attractive and vigorous presence
Cassius Clay, with whom I exchanged plethoric, intense words at the
Faculty Club of the University of Puerto Rico where I was at that time
professor of literature
And Eugène Boch, the Belgian poet who remains alive in the
portrait painted by Van Gogh, with a halo of twinkling little stars as
background

Cyrano earnestly meandered through a tightly packed tiny bookstore
In his elegant, delicious old Caribbean town
He feasted on covers, caressed odd titles
Impeccable actor, his talent glowed in the way he moved, the way
he carried himself, such as the engaging words that to Roxanne he
spoke in the film

Sometime later I gazed enraptured at his sculpted image that
masterfully reflected that very hard to come by transition between
child or youth
Part of a handsome group sculpture adorning the family pantheon in

5

the Island's most celebrated cemetery, Santa Magdalena de Pazzis
Here the worthy rest lulled by the open sea on one side, while on
another the famously infamous slum, privileged by its picturesque
site and name: "La Perla" ("The Pearl)," remains a paean to the
inhabitants' unique sense of mirth

There it is!
Immortality no less
Movies, sculpture, memory guard the personality of a genuine star in
the great stage that is the world

A few years later I came back anticipating the permanence of what I
thought a priceless, indelible portrait
I found instead all sorts of body parts: arms, hands, legs, torsos,
decapitated heads; the sculptures, sadly torn asunder, lay strewn all
over the ground

My imbecile desire became humus for the ardently desired remains
Oh vandals of the Caribbean, how dare you!
"Ozymandias" lives once more, I said to myself
"Look on my works, ye mighty, and despair!"

I fell asleep again
This time Derek Walcott appeared in my dreams
Extraordinary deep blue eyes, framed by his salty, dark skin, sailed
forth as did his words from "Omeros": "I sang our wide country, the
Caribbean Sea," comforting me to the point I was ready to leave the
familiar despair of the voyager behind in order to embark on new
ventures

Tonight I awoke with Bob Dylan in my bed
Neither cranky nor aloof
Experienced and passionate
He made love to me
His lady of the Islands

Sometimes a fantasy can heal
Sometimes a fantasy can make you whole
Sometimes a fantasy is so like reality
Sometimes a dream is true

Yesterday I visited "The Potato Eaters"
The light of a humble kerosene lamp paid homage to the struggle for
life
While it fitfully illuminated the coarse, wrinkled faces, the hands
made rough by excess labor and the hard earned pitiful sustenance
The splendid shine of ochers, gold and browns strengthened me to
the point that I felt
There is no need to rage against the dying of the light.

———

Bio: *(María Arrillaga)* Widely published, María Arrillaga writes poetry, fiction, essays, literary criticism and is a specialist in gender studies. Recent publications: Ciudades como mares – poetry 1966-1993 2010, Isla Negra, and Flamigos en San Juan/Flamingos in Manhattan, 2010, Puerto Editors. Both books are bilingual. Maña Valentina, novel, Cuarto Propio, Chile, was finalist in contest sponsored by Institute of Latin American Writers, NY, 1996.

Madeline Artenberg

Clam Lady

For two years, I passed you on Sixth and forty-fifth,
dumping water over your yellow-nailed feet,
chasing down clams with Nathan's dogs—
always in the same flowered shift
the wind lifted above
your gray knees.

Then, last month, I saw you
in the Duane Reade, sporting
mink and a French twist.
What got you up off the corner?
You reached the front of the checkout—
bought "Love that Red" lipstick,
raced into the crowd before I could follow.

Big-boned, blood-faced woman,
today, you're back
on the same corner—
no makeup.

Clam Lady, please speak.
Tell me, every morning at six,
the butler brings
your seaside favorites, tucks
a napkin under your chin,
pries open
the first shell.

_____

Bio: *(Madeline Artenberg)* **Madeline Artenberg's poetry has appeared in many print and online publications, such as Vernacular and Rattle. She won Lyric Recovery and Poetry Forum prizes and was semi-finalist in the 2005 contest of Margie, The American Journal of Poetry. The play, The Old In-and-Out, based on her poetry and Karen Hildebrand's, directed by Kat Georges, garnered raves in June, 2013.**

Carmen Bardeguez-Brown

Bang Bang

Bang Bang
Writing a futuristic poem of events that
Would have taken place by January 1,2014
Yes,
You heard that right.
Iam writing the poem today
On a cold Friday evening of October 25,2013
What could possibly happen in the next 67 days?
I know
It's going to be a lot colder
Yes, colder than the 41 degrees
A lottttttttttttt colder

Bang
bang
Republicans will try to defund Obamacare.
Bang
Yes they will try it again

Bang bang

Obama will continue to be accused of being
Too liberal
Too conservative
Too communist
Too capitalist
Too Muslim
Too Christian
Too humanitarian
Too imperialist
Too black
Too white
To to to to
To to to to

Bang
Too much of this
Too much of that
Reality TV continues to make ways into the American vulture,culture
landscape
Bang
The tea party continues to be the bunker of fascist racist mostly
white American males.
Bang
Toooooooo much tttttttttooooooooo much
Tooooooo muchhhhhhh tttttooooooo much
Bang bang
Ayyyyyyyyy. Dios mio tuuuuuuuu mucho pendeja. Bang

Jennifer Blowdryer

Smooth Nothin'

I never would have thought Rick Savage would appear cute to me, similar to a collectible, but at the non-event opening for yet another restaurant, there he was, along with a rogue's gallery of other aging perverts. The difference between a neurotic and a pervert, it is said, is that perverts have the ability to act on their impulses. It counts. I've seen Rick Savage in old video porn, slapping a sappy looking woman's tits against a bar tying them up with rope until they turn blue, using a pair of pliers to juggle the nipple up and down. Of course this is no way to behave, not in the world of propriety, but this didn't stop Rick Savage, the cameraman, or even the women from carrying on and on in this manner.

"Can I have your autograph!" I gushed. "Sure", he replied, looking not at all psycho. "Do you still run those festivals?"

Mr. Savage was referring to my Smut Fests of yore, and it turned out that Lenny, from Hellfire, remembered them too.

"No, now that there's burlesque everywhere, I don't feel the same imperative" I honestly replied. So true.

Once urbanites hid their shady pasts, now a young performance artist is fully capable of inventing one. To be authentic, like a curry sauce. Like a youngish vagabond, carrying a pet ferret, still bearing a whiff of a future. Not like a stew bum, eyes ragged, desperate to talk or stay silent, scarfing down the beet salad at frittata at the Catholic Worker, on First Street between First and Second Avenue, 3 doors up from Prune, where strangers go to savor the excellent cuisine, smoothie/colonics establishment another 3 doors down, where presumably they encourage patrons to transcend the earthly coil of appetite by charging $8.75 for a small bottle of grapefruit juice.

"Does it have special properties?" I once asked, holding the expensive plastic bottle of juice up to the light.

"It's organic," replied the counterperson, stuck working there and without the gift of gab that peddling elixirs should always require. Once a freelance wine salesman on the Upper East Side said this cheap Russian wine on sale had 'geological properties' and it was all I could do not to just hand him all my money straight away.

Some other relics of perversion attended the opening at 69 Gansevoort, the former address of a late night restaurant called Florent. The Staff of The Vault, a horrible so called dungeon at 14th Street and 9th Avenue, would repair to Florent to chuckle over the clientele and their own continued survival, including my roguish friend Mistress Veronica, who was a House Dom at The Vault. She compared it to being a crazed recreation director, and of course one knew immediately what she meant. Oh, the squishy passivity of the male masochist of a certain age. Makes you want to slug them. Which is their point. Not mine.

Steve Cannon

Drones

Big (Daddy)
Data
Drones
Smart Phones
Tones
Who's watching Who
Or better yet
Who's listening to Who
Big Data
But does it really matter

Patricia Carragon

Model Call

model call:

free coloring at a tony salon near the hi-line, going from "blah" to "beautiful," "looking hot" for at least a week, 2 ½ hours of intensive analysis & instruction, free chemical sorcery—all in the pseudonym of beauty.

my roots, a stubborn mixture, the color of shit tainted with aluminum, copper, & gold, date back to my college years. deeper still . . . & much harder to conceal, my working class roots on the class-conscious catwalk.

my day off, my day for beauty, my day for deep-rooted trouble! the instructor, a tall, 99% fat-free blonde, examined my roots. she didn't want to hear about my approved status. my roots were unfit for the beginners' class & my name should be removed from the list. but, since I've made the long trip down, her "bitchiness" allowed me to stay.

Among the 20-something students were the older ones—the ones who own salons, the ones who've dealt with roots like mine

shit hit my working class roots! i shared my disgust with my assigned student, a salon owner— she offered to speak with the instructor. minutes later, the receptionist asked to speak with me in private.

shit hit my working class roots! deemed disruptive, i was asked to leave.

model call:

my day off, my day for beauty uprooted! my working class roots sashayed off the class-conscious catwalk—my vowel movement stank with shit!

15

the tall, 99% fat-free blonde smiled as the elevator's steel door closed.

karma should kick her ass!

Mary Elizabeth Clark

La Tienda - Impressions From South California

to walk along the quiet street
      amid the hush and pom
      of unfamiliar flowers

where tiny hummers mummed about
      the canterbury bells

phoebus raying torid glory
      hearts of crested light and gold

from up the holy zenith, of
      a still and cloudless sky

to enter then, a shadey place
      a store of wickered baskets
      candle jars and lanterns
      and brightly colored tins

a sleepy kitten stalking through
      the landscape of a dreams caprice

napped in the warp and lag
      of a quiet old tienda

i paid a pennyworth for peaches
      and tucked them in a paper sack

the high pacific sun inclining
> through an open door
> advanced the heat
> and moment
> rise
> of a shadowless noon

———

Bio: *(Mary Elizabeth Clark)* Mary Elizabeth Clark is a new york city poet, living in brooklyn. she has a background in teaching and the performing arts. some of her work has been represented in journals including: the villager ; mobius; poetz.com and roguescholars.com. she has been a featured reader at some local venus such as the cornelia street cafe; scali's; and the nightingale.

John Clinton

Palm Sunday

God
could be
seen in the sun
blindness is faith
for every moment
could be beautiful
birds will always sing
regardless of the weather
inhaling every second
exhaling every time
witnesses to evolution
in the concrete jungle
hibernating hipsters howl
in the mirror, cracking open
infinite sky to infinite sea
in the male to female
sharing of an orange
peeled like an ape
eaten like an intellectual
a significant shift
in the paradigm of affinity
spanning bridges & boroughs
absinthe bars & basements
a dry holy season spent
in exile on Metropolitan Avenue
Mama, they're gonna crucify me!
drifting on Palm Sunday
in dirty leather boots
where the wild things are
home is where mother
nature is, the heart
is an organ peel
carefully & consume
the skin of the sun

beating Brooklyn
to a bloody pulp
now drink
God up
& see

_____

Bio: *(John Clinton)* John Clinton was born & raised in Brooklyn, NY. He graduated from the School of Visual Arts where he studied filmmaking. He has been published in Nomad's Choir & Great Weather for Media's recent anthology, The Understanding between Foxes & Light. He currently resides in Staten Island, NY.

Abby Coleman

Innate

When I say *I love Beyoncé* you say *Why? I
love Beyoncé because she is the body I want
the inside of my eyelids to be when I'm dead*

Jess Cording

Sleeping Strange

What I wouldn't do to whittle this down
to a favored fever dream.

When excuses sound like reasons
I remember the storm of adrift
and grasping for salt
when I'm over my head under ocean.

I'm patient like a lit match,
a straight-backed question mark
in a black dress.

The ice in my handshake
doesn't stand a chance
in this heart attack of a hiding place.

I sleep strange sometimes, wake up looking
for a death mask beside me in bed,
a man smiling like maybe
he forgot.

I'm not asking for anyone
to look me in the eye and tell me
which water cradles the wreck
I swim through
when I close my eyes and look around.

I'd just like some warning
about that snake in the grass
and the sparks I can't stamp out,
something to remind me
a cautionary tale always tastes like invitation.

Steve Dalachinsky

Faces On The Wall

we live in the faces on the wall
in the drum within the soul
of the dancer
in the skuttle & the tap & the
boogie woogie
heartbeats

we sing with the arts within our blood
as the hood of the sky shelters us
from demons & stars
we walk on the waters of life &
fall apart in its presence
like shy little kids by the campfire

we scat in time's trunk
& break the chains of life
we fold like flowers
like old linen like old paper & old scotch
fold into ourselves like notes
we live within the monsters & the mothers
of the world
fold into ourselves like notes

we devour our breakfast
we devour our lunch
we devour our dinner
we devour our ancestors
we live in the faces on the wall
embraced by the shawl of winter
kissed by the lips of spring
haunted by the rhythms of summer
devoured by the colors of fall
while we devour our children
devour the lives on the wall
fill our eyes with rainwater
& abandon ourselves to the light

JM Theisen de Gonzalez

Matchless

I would actually like to dedicate this to a lot of exes that I met online.

I'll start with the homeless guy who was living out of his car; the crazy psychologist who told me it was okay to drink alcohol while taking Topamax for migraines, and claimed to sleep with a lot of celebrities that he did not know were celebrities until after someone told him; the government employee who informed me that my insomnia was due to an insufficient belief in God, to trust that He would wake me up the next day; the guy who apparently romanced a whole group of women and once he made his pick, dumped the rest of us by telling us what our "faults" were, when he signed us all up for spam email in closing.

I thought I might write about my last Match.com guy --the site that claims to "find love, guaranteed"? I should have thought twice when the dude found out that I worked in a specific theatre, and the night that we were "dark", security found him pounding on the door because he "wanted to meet" me. There was no show that night, they told him, so he went home to email me and tell me this. Call me willing to give a second chance, or foolish, but I did agree to meet him. He seemed harmless enough.

So a few dates in, during dinner, he announces he needs a cigarette, which is a complete surprise to me, a non-smoker looking for the same as I clearly stated in my profile. He told me he was "quitting". Well, right about now, this man seems like a really bad idea. I tried breaking up with him. He tells me it's "too soon".

I eventually decide that we'll try a "sleepover date" at his new place. As I exit the elevator, I look around and I see a tiny toy stuffed squirrel in a dress propped up against his apartment door. "Isn't she CUTE!" he exclaimed. That wasn't her only appearance of the night. In the bed--dead center of the pillows. That precipitated the next breakup discussion in which I was told I was "dropping the whammy on him" and "this was entirely unexpected." That conversation also led to the disclosure that he lived around the corner from his psychiatrist whom he paid $14,000 a year out-of-pocket to see. So, unfortunately ,like it or not, I still had a boyfriend.I attempted one more time to end things, and this time I was told: "I cannot accept this as a decision."

This was seeming a bit like an exercise in futility until one afternoon, I finally had had enough and simply went over to his apartment and told him I was breaking up with him, not to be negotiated or discussed further, which of course led to thirty-seven phone messages on my answering machine that began with "I know you don't want to talk to me...". Even the one mentioning the detectives from my precinct contacting him about the excessive phone messages. Of course, he called to make sure that it wasn't me that called the police.

and finally, sex with a narcissist? Worst 3-way EVER!

Vivian Demuth

Ode To The Veggie-oil Car

(For Lee)

The fragrance of gas
station pumps,
putrid,
grows like fire in summer
before the open road
that is a highway man
who torments
gasoline drivers
working 3 jobs
and the car-less
unemployed.
Scorched cities,
cooking from
climate-change heat
drag
us down,
bite us in the belly
while napping
in shakey, air-conditioned
buses
dreaming of
cool lakes
with shady bars &
of driving clean
veggie-oil
fueled cars.
You, veggie-oil car,
are the designer
jewelry of the
diesel mind.
The edible sex
of rabbit

volkswagons,
& 4x4's.
In a carbon-bloated universe,
You, zero emissions traveler,
guzzle leftovers,
canola or corn,
that dissolve into pure
energy,
orgasmic delight
that we too
consume.
Queen of grease,
we want to rub
our frazzled hair in your
olive oil,
bury our fear
in your odourless
possibilities &
your recycled
soul.
Among our longings
to save our wallets &
ourselves,
You, veggie-oil car,
are a beacon of
green
light, solar-powered
that illuminates
alternative
roads.
And that is why you
don't pollute us
in these
super-storm
climes.
You just
slide by
with your
genius
shared at

greasecar.com,
while each new
hurricane
is a reminder of
a future that will include
your cars or no cars,
your people or whatever
else is beyond
our human ability to
imagine.

_____

Bio: *(Vivian Demuth)* Vivian Demuth is a poet and fiction writer whose work has appeared in various journals and anthologies in Canada, the United States, Mexico, and Europe. She is the author of an ecological novel, Eyes of the Forest (Smoky Peace Press, 2007), and a new book of poetry, Fire Watcher (Guernica Editions, 2013).

Gabriel Don

candy in my fingertips

                               smile
but i was raised
by a dragon
and
if
you
mess
with my
babies
watch me breathe fire
have one foot on the ground
but i was raised by a witch
watch me
        make
              magic

———

Bio: *(Gabriel Don)* **Gabriel Don received her MFA in Fiction at The New School, where she worked as the chapbook and reading series coordinator. Her work has appeared in The Brooklyn Rail, Short Fast and Deadly, A Minor and Westerly. She has appeared in visual poems such as Woman Without Umbrella and Unbound. She started several reading-soiree series and is editorial staff at LIT.**

Tessa Lou Fix

Organic Heroin

These shoes in and out of me
like the organically grown heroin I do- now I will do no other.
Pesticide free coco fields crowd my mind these days
swimming across the South America of my heart
jamming at my borders and sinews like a Colombian cartel wet
dream
pounding at my uterine wall till I give birth to a soft white kilo?

My thighs press together like a thousand non genetically engineered
poppy fields
my conscience
like the Arab nations where these dreams are sown
falls to the ground (the bathroom floor).
An Afghanistan of the soul, so to speak

Here we kill without thinking
a discrimination so high it reaches beyond any type
of normal morality.
Wait! Don't say that!
I mean there is no killing here!
No taxing on Al Qaeda and addiction.
This is a cruelty free war zone

grass fed only goats traffic my dope
across the Mexico line
I shoot with pride...
sweet sweet Chiba of my countries memory banks.
These days I lie in wait of what you may bring me next
the barbaric pressures of
what its like to be tortured
by water boards and such,
whatever uh tortured
uncut democracies, drug free school zones and AIDS
come for the golden egg.

Oh please do it with your blessed amulets,
pre cooked cases of synthetic earth and rocks!
Oh,come on, freebase like it's another time...

1982 and the epidemic is new.
We kill for a...hit
(White) women on the street
tied to their ankles, open hearted crying for it

you mean dead on the front page. Back page.

Heroin and memory.
Memory and baby as
an epidemic crashes our streets.
Only we are self made- our teenage nation
a plague of forgiveness like intimations ...ghetto 1, ghetto 2
buckle my shoe...
ghetto 1 -- a Jew
ghetto 2-- black and blue-

Forever I love you.

_____

Bio: *(Tessa Lou Fix)* **Tessa Lou Fix is an artist, poet and scholar. She resides in NYC where she was born, however she escapes to the Mohawk River Valley where she has space to think, write and play with her son in the corn fields. Her punk wearable art clothing line can be found on TessaLou.net. Her work has been shown in various NY galleries in Chelsea including the Chelsea Hotel and the Lyons Weir Gallery, as well as doing readings and performances at the local NYC haunts. She was recently featured in art mag, spassian.is and is currently working on a multi media project about abandonment connected to the Holocaust and forgotten Jewish histories. Her short book White Trash Lesbian, a Post Sandy Illusion is on the way.**

Robert Gibbons

The Mayan Apocalypse

my grandma had been crying for years it's going to rain;
she said, God told Noah it's going to rain, but it will not
be water, but fire next time; it will not be her, but me
next time my mortal flesh will dissolve into dust,
call the society and have them to bury my bones near
King Osceola or near King Tupac; bury me in the freedom
of the ancestors; portal my frame into the winter haven of
Florida; bury me near Peru or the Andes, near the
volcano of Craig Arnold, or the vat of King Christophe;
but let me crystallize; allow me to realize; and if
the time comes let it be of Gregorian Chant,
for I want the moan of the monks; the fugue of Bach,
want the subtle sounds of Couperin or the gospel of Georgia;
want to die to flesh; want to run into the vestment of a
cypress swamp and hide with Blessed and Zora;
for this is still wilderness, this is not religious; it's liberation
in the sanctified bones of my people; and they are native,
and are as sacred as this poem.

Daniela Gioseffi

Earth's Body In True Genesis

Meteorites and comets delivered carbons from outer space to her
smoldering surface. Carbons full of amino acids seeded Her—
proteins of life from dust of stars in balls of ice smashed into Her:
some big as mountains; others small as pebbles, exploded as they
slammed into Her moldering mass creating *petides.*

The leap to life began in deep sulfuric caverns where bacteria first
blossomed, sucking energy from sub-surfaces where heavens
of microbes flourished, living on exotic diets of gases, methane,
sulfur…

DNA erupted from oceans, where chemicals inside Her forming soil
spewed into warm waters, feeding to bloom life, as a half billion
years ago, meteorites and comets stopped their big bombardment—

She cooled as immense colonies of green slime fed by the sun and
photosynthesis began, spreading vegetation

over the cooling surface of Her mass
still spinning from the first huge explosion.
Forests were formed up and down mountain peaks and valleys of
Her early beginning. In the hills of oceans of *stromatelites* where
sticky cells of bacteria migrated to tops of rocks to live as microbes
and drink sun. Cities of tiny bacteria lived reaching up

out of Her shallow waters breathing out oxygen, combining with iron
in the Age of Rust. Layers of oxide built streams of iron ore on floors
of Her primordial oceans.

Cyanobacteria, blue-green algae breathed out oxygen filling Her
atmosphere, overpowering noxious gases so living creatures could
endure. A layer of ozone ascended as a veil over Her. Then came
fish, reptiles, insects, birds, primates and, finally, humans in the last
few "moments." Now, here we are in all our complexity, murdering

each other over an unborn God.

All our art, music, poetry, religions have not stopped the carnage
as She melts in the sun and Her oceans rise to drown coastal
communities and destroy us.

One day, when we've stopped wasting our energy on bloody
weaponry we will turn and look
into the children's eyes and be inspired, seeing these newborn
angels, as the only real angels born of Her, we will let "God" who is
actually "Love" be fully born. Then,

the angels made of stardust, made of carbon, hydrogen, oxygen, will
build new homes in the universe where other life blooms to befriend,
and there, maybe then, devoid of fossil fuels and carbon pollution,
"God" will finally exist as Earth's body.

———

Bio: *(Daniela Gioseffi)* Daniela Gioseffi, American Book Award winner
of 16 books of poetry and prose, has won NY State Council for the Arts
grants, The John Ciardi Lifetime Achievement Award in poetry, and edits
www.Eco-Poetry.org/ on Climate Crisis. She's presented on NPR, BBC-radio
and worldwide at major book fairs and universities. Her verse is etched on
a wall of PENN Station, NY.

Jane B. Grenier

Anthrax And Bombs

Everybody's worried about Anthrax and Bombs, weapons of mass destruction are an unseen scare.

The frightening reality of a chemical war nightmare.

The dreaded threat that can harm us all, when the bombs hit, we are all gonna fall.

Well check this out... You plug it in, spray it on, roll it over, dab it behind your ears, between your legs or up your pits, you even hang those awful evergreen trees in a bag from a string on your automobile's rear view mirror.

You smear on your smell so nice, your old fuckin' spice, you tidy your bowl, lysol your cold, lemon fresh your glade, shout out your stains, flush 'em down the drain, and don't forget to bounce your mutha-fuckin' dryer!

So yes I know …

Everybody's worried about anthrax and bombs, but I'm here to tell you that it's YOU that I fear, all that smell that you smear on daily from your toes up to your hair.

Chemical warfare ain't no foreign threat...   You dig?

It's comes from much closer to home than you think.

So let me break it down for your smelly old self.

It's chemical warfare every time you buy the shit that's on their shelf.

You're like a junkie on a fix with chemicals habits that you feed pluggin', dabbin', washin', rinsin', sprayin', smearin', rollin' up, between your legs, or in your pits, or anywhere you feel the need, but you tell me... who the terrorist be?

You got leaf blowers and suv's, smelly skidoos and leaky jet skis. Air fresheners plugged into every wall... febreezing you all, and gadgets for every thought. All battery powered worlds from can 'till can't, sucking energy from a wire that goes to...WHAT?

The electric plant.

Electricity...like magic...it comes from the sky... or gods... or fairies... IT just IS. Don't ask why.

What are you stupid? Just where do you think plastic comes from?

Ever heard of petroleum? From oil it does come.

And while we're on the subject of stupid, let's move right along to our beloved television, big brothers delivery system, erasing all visions with nothing to see or think about.

A *Bergeron box that will drown your soul steel your brain make you old before your time, litter your mind, with trash, like you litter the planet with disposable lighters, and diapers and things I wouldn't even begin to know about.

How you gonna buy some shit, unwrap it and without a blink toss it on the ground?

Ever heard of Mother Earth? How you gonna get her dirty for the babies you birth?

You stupid motha fuckas have you no clue? You gotta watch just what you do.

You're like a junkie on a fix with personal habits that you feed, without regard to the Mother

you need... you Need... you NEED!

So the next time you're checking out of your local food mart, take a good long look in your own shopping cart.
Then you tell me... who the terrorist be!

(*Bergeron: character in the short story "Harrison Bergeron" by Kurt Vonnegut, Jr.)

Bob Hart

So He Saw Me!

Death was sneaking in the shadows near my door.
"Come in" I said. "Don't be shy."
He said: "I saw you kiss them – schmooze them
before they woke to so-called workaday:
the mothers husbands kids and their kittens.
Are you so much in love with the living?"
"Fond" I answered "of their actual lives and
potentials; sad that they so much are
solely moment to seed the figure of fauna."
"Aha" spoke Death (sun and shade
leafy-fluttering on his emptiness)
and whose was that hand I saw held yours
as you smoochily trespassed all their sleeping?"
"An essence as thin as you my grey friend
and steeper. A racer smart and swift and
passionate: gamesomely named Immortality."

Stephanie Hart

In The Dark

In 1955 when I was six, my father lifted me up on his shoulders to get a good look at the Christmas tree at Rockefeller Center. The lights looked like multicolored stars drawing a picture in the dark. My father murmured, "That tree will be here even when life gets mean and ugly."

My parents divorced the next year, and I went to boarding school. While we never visited the tree again as a family, it lived on in my imagination. As an adult I would visit it every year, always in the evening. The year my father died, the lights took on his playful, angry energy; at my mother's death, her capacity to shine. The year the World Trade Center imploded before my eyes, the tree shone with renewed brilliance. This year as I walked up behind it, the lights cast a blue mist almost like rain. I turned toward the angels. Their trumpets were raised, piping unheard music into the dark.

Bob Heman

Salad Days

There is much to do to be a father.
You move the blade casually to your left hand.
Even after the ceremony the aches did not end.
She sighed and shoved away the plate of beets.
You alter the arrangement slightly.
The man with the derby is sighing again.
There are five eggs left in the refrigerator.
And then there was the one about the baby who forgot to cry.
The envelope was half an inch too short.
Your dog always had a passion for carrots.
It was not easy for her to adjust either.
You always thought that it blurred the eyes.
She told you her underwear was too tight.
The paper said nothing about the air crash in Peru.
Suddenly it began to snow.
The man with the derby taps you on the shoulder.
She just couldn't make it get hard.
Do you remember how to play marbles.
No one could be seen in the viewfinder of the camera.
Tomorrow is her birthday.
She tasted a small slice of cheese.
You discovered that water is made of oxygen and hydrogen.
I touched her ear gently with my tongue.
The night became very cool.
Perhaps he didn't know any better.
Whenever she was nervous she'd wash the ashtrays.
He felt that he understood blood.
The man with the derby rattled his newspaper violently.
She told me I made her nervous.

(*First published in "The Mid Atlantic Review")

———

Bio: *(Bob Heman)* **Bob Heman has edited CLWN WR (formerly Clown War) since the early 1970s. His e-books How It All Began and Demographics, or, The Hats They Are Allowed to Wear are available as free downloads from Quale Press.**

Aimee Herman

An Examination Of Collapsible Tent Or Nomadic Bone Structure

There is no permanence when home is found in nooks of humans. If you call her a wanderer, then at least you are paying attention to the flap of lashes slowing down. Sleep *here* for a night. *Here* is defined by Pluto and that cold beast no longer exists so this is why you are sleep-deprived. A new woman with lap and highly educated tongue tries to court your childhood away. And maybe your queer is defined by who you spread your legs to but mine is defined by bookshelves and the way my brain gathers when I'm near them. Far from view, where only fires get a drift of that strumming pattern, a human searches for oars big enough to paddle through ocean of birds. Imagine winged water. Imagine salted teeth that heal with each bite. Yesterday, a man grabbed my arm in order to read the drip of skin that is unscarred. That reminds me, I cannot afford this, but there will always be nineteen cent noodles and edible mushrooms that grow in freezers and I can suck the sweat from my hair when there is no water left. Or you can build a bridge with your newly gathered gender, strength of army. And although war may be collecting on the other sides of this, a body finally surrenders and walks alone toward the truth of what existed all along.

Diana Gitesha Hernandez

Fly Breed

We are dying
Alonso
Sabes es la verdad
Solitude on the street
Is like a bitter fruit
A nasty seed
But in this kitchen
Nada exists
Along side
The daily numbers game

Beans and drifting dreams
Heart's an island
Body a shore
City scaping eyes that spy
Grey tall
Nothings'
Left to calculate
It doesn't add up
Does it, but wait

A fluid stream of air
Close your eyes
Feel the body
Coming undone
Letting mind slip

Kate Irving

Dust Jacket Blurb

It's all about living in a hallway
where everything is divided into its
place at either end. To access what
exists, a center path has been worn
into a trough darkened by scuff
marks – years of her shoes and
sloughed off cells from the soles of
her feet; a trough made slippery with
flung sweat, spit spent on swears,
bloodstain and occasional rain
where the roof is in disrepair. From
windows, numbered by decade,
permanent and non-permanent faces
review the continuing process. This
reviewer found mirrors at both ends
confusing, images repeated with
undisciplined imagination. In pursuit
of some outcome or reduction in
trajectory, the author often stops
at mid-point, waiting to get hit,
forgetting she is the projectile, that
the act of holding the poles apart is
everything.

Evie Ivy

The Girls And Their Savings

They're saving men, two pretty girls down the sidewalk
Are saving men. We do need them in paradise.
One has a straight blond pony tail and a brunet
With long wavy hair, are giving out religious tracts
With invitations to the church. "How do you do?"
"Please come, and be saved" they are saying to the men—
Young men and still healthy looking middle aged men.
The girls talk and they giggle. "Come to the service!"
I walk behind them a few blocks, before I enter
A store, and had noticed they didn't offer one
To the ladies, younger or older that passed them by.
We do need those good looking men in paradise,
(And I think, who would want their husband in that church?)
On my way home an older woman gives me a tract.

I then wondered if it was the same church, because
The girls are happily saving men. And praise the Lord.
Up the avenue they walk, and they're saving men.

———

Bio: *(Evie Ivy)* Evie Ivy is a dancer/poet in the NYC poetry circuit. Producer
of the "Dance of the Word" programs, a fusion of poetry and dance. Host of
the long running Green Pavilion Poetry Event, in Brooklyn, whose second
anthology, "The Venetian Hour . . . Dinner with the Muse Vol. II" should
already be available. She teaches the art of Belly Dancing.

C. D. Johnson

Missed Connection

You, a Korean woman, shoulder length brown hair, blue raincoat,
gold purse,
eyes like sad cool puddles on a forest floor at night with the
moonlight dancing in the ripples.

Me, a black man, shaved head, grey t-shirt, jeans and work boots,
gray backpack,
good-looking in a African American Jason Statham sort of way.

> [Time: The 1st second.]

I was holding onto the overhead crossbar on the train with one hand,
and reading from copies of the Brahma Sutras in the other.

In the dinginess of the subway window as we passed through the
tunnel,
I saw you eyeing me from the side as you clung to a vertical pole.

At first,
your stare seemed clinical;

but I watched as you examined my arm reaching up to the crossbar.

You looked downward,
your eyes skipping across the outer frame,
my ribs and my legs.

A smile leaked from the corner of your mouth as you began to focus
on other areas.

Ladies are taught as girls not to stare at these- -openly.

Watching you in the glass,
I noticed the way your rain coat pulled away from you as you rocked

back and forth with the movement of the train car.
Your v-neck was classy,
though its application bordered on bad-girl chic.

It rode close to risque territory,
coming within a hair's breath of divulging secrets.

No bra could be seen through the blue and yellow material of your
blouse;

you chose to go "fancy free" that today.

There was an ever so slight variation of skin color showing through
the fabric- -on certain "arcs".

Finally, you looked forward -
our eyes meeting in the window.

You were caught.

You turned away.

I turned in your direction,
smiling;

then bending my head down,
I went back to my papers.

Out of my peripheral vision,
I could see you staring again.

I looked back at the window,
and there you were.

Eye contact.

I turned again and smiled.

You smiled back.

You giggled a little,
then turned away again,
betraying your inner flirt.

In that one moment,
I wondered about how you would decorate our apartment -
and what kind of dog we'd adopt together.

The train stopped.

Newport Station.

You moved towards me to get off.

Walking behind me,
your arm grazes my back-
There was plenty of room for you to pass clear of me without
touching.

I watched as you left the train and headed up the platform stairs.

Just before you disappeared out of view,
you skewed your hair behind your ear with your hand and watched
my reaction.

One last bit of play.

The doors of the train closed shut,
and as the train moved away and we separated,
I voiced quietly under breath one word:

"Damn."

        [Time: 48 seconds later.]

Simply not enough time.

———

Bio: *(C. D. Johnson)* C. D. Johnson was formally editor-in-chief of Rogue Scholars Press which published hundreds of poets from the New York City East Village poetry community, both online and in print, between 1997 and 2009. As a professional "Mr. Spock", when he's not teaching small business owners how to navigate the technological age, he spends his spare time instructing impressionable young minds in logic, analytical philosophy, and Vedanta.

Ice Gayle Johnson

Rage Defines Behavior-the Purse Dream

Rage- defines behavior.
History manages the insanity.

Loud screams expose the story
shame drapes a black veil-

it drips and melts away truths;
we stand naked in daylight

deny all(pain dips into the belly)
creates recurring diseases

the news doesn't report damage
the news never- never reports

this kind of damage, all we can do-
is scream in silence

explosions pop and blow
then the effects of silence exposes-

itself- blood guts eyes wide
open-and we know the rest of the

nightmare where the dream
takes control and here we are once

again- it's always a new and confusing
scenario distraught and out of sorts

out of my bed feverishly I search
the room to find my purse,

grab it from the chair hold it close to my chest-
I know this purse!

Boni Joi

Insomnia Mad Libs

Sleep today in the indigo ideas of clouds
better then being asleep in a sentence

or at the wheel,
or on a subway at 2am with all the dosing men
and the girl trying to steady herself on 5 inch heels
after 2 martinis and 3 vodka sodas with friends
nice that subway cars have poles.

This used to be the city that never sleeps
and now it's just you that doesn't.

Drink melatonin-rich cherry juice
train yourself to fall asleep
with a Pavlovian ritual
such as rubbing your belly
or your nose in a circular motion.

If it works for small furry animals why shouldn't it work for you?

Think of what you did in this morning
and recall the rest of your day.
This may cause you to screech
or make you tired.

Limit your alcohol intake and exercise
block racing brain with white noise.

Do not contemplate the following sentences:

The Labrador screening will be better than the screening in the labs

They woke up for breakfast and found their cars were toast

Or questions like:
Is my online presence as good as my actual presence?

These are not sleepy sentences
they are full of more questions

envisioning the meaning of
colorless green ideas sleep furiously
will surely induce sleep

as will *New York bison New York bison bully bully New York bison*
poets know *the exquisite corpse will drink the new wine*

curiously deep, the slumber of crimson thoughts.

(*Notes: The last two lines on page one are from the New York Post. Colorless green ideas sleep furiously was written by Noam Chomsky as an example of a nonsensical grammatically correct sentence. Curiously deep, the slumber of crimson thoughts was written by John Hollander from the poem Coiled Alizarin dedicated to Noam Chomsky. The third to last line in the poem is a manifestation of the sentence Buffalo Buffalo buffalo Buffalo buffalo buffalo buffalo Buffalo buffalo by William J. Rapaport, professor emeritus at University at Buffalo showing how homophones and homonyms can be used to construct sentences. The exquisite corpse will drink the new wine was the first nonsensical sentence generated by the surrealist game of cadavre exquis (1925), the game was named after the sentence.)

Larry Jones

darling devil derring-do

(a song)
(melody)

yes those days one pays
the devil his full due
and then the handsome devil
goes all the way for you

the devil you say really
the devil i say i do
the devil you say maybe
laughter all for you

(refrain)

laughter loves you devil
jesus loves you too
forty-plus years of hell
fire what can feel so true

devil made me do it
devil make me do
do me darling devil
darling devil derring-do

(refrain)

lovely devil dashing now
about to do me wrong
darling devil just for you
i sing this little song

(refrain)

yes darling devil
yes darling devil
yes darling devil
yes jesus loves you too

———

Bio: *(Larry Jones)* Larry Jones was the co-producer with Bruce Weber of the first ANYDSWPE at Café Nico, his loft apartment and poetry/ performance art project above the Pyramid Club, in 1995. He is an Associate of the Academy of American Poets, and his biography appears in Marquis Who's Who in America. He teaches in the Saturday Classes for Young People program at Hostra University.

Eliot Katz

Death And War

On the last car of a late night N train
I asked Death how it managed
        to move so quickly
                during wars.

"I'm not sure why," Death answered,
"but ever since Hiroshima
        my skates glide faster
                over the cool Earth."

I asked whether it was possible
to tell the difference
        between a civilian
                and a young draftee.

"No difference."

I said from my own perspective
there was at least something different
        about a playful child struck
                by remote-control drone or stray cluster bomb.

Death glared between my eyes.

I debated with Death about the merits
of a bullet, a car crash, & a baseball bat--
        It confessed the first case
                of pediatric AIDS

had almost bounced back & shocked Death
        to death.

Approaching the last stop, I asked
whether it ever thought,

despite a difficult economy,
        to look for an easier job.

Death laughed & pointed to the front page
of today's New York Times.
        "Watch your step, E. Katz,
                but don't make it obvious."

———

Bio: *(Eliot Katz)* **Eliot Katz is the author of seven poetry books, including Unlocking the Exits; and Love, War, Fire, Wind: Looking Out from North America's Skull. His most recent publications are two 2013 prose e-books: Three Radical Poets: Tributes to Allen Ginsberg, Gregory Corso, and Adrienne Rich; and The Moonlight of Home and Other Stories of Truth and Fiction.**

Amy King

Back To The Future Is My Endgame

The government's social media is upon us.
It's hard to say which is either,
it's hard to notice if I am neither,
it's hard to tell what's more worthy,
even in content-specific instances.
I mean, are we not full of money
and filling up on wild boar meat?
Do we not pet the goat and steal their oil?
We are not the same rotten filling that comes
from donut holes, but we do dash
here and then there and then some
just to get noticed. As in, notice that I am not you;
I'm the one who thinks of you every other orgasm,
at least, just to make sense of this contagion
we call today. Self-study, self masturbatory, self immolation,
self mirroring peckish parrots to hear you.
So next level. Adjust the preceding language
to become the one you most admire.
They used to call it single white female –
but now we call it "there is anti-matter there"
beyond that umbilical horizon of Ethernets,
or in Lacanian speak – there is no portside.
But I'm the rabbit calling your name
through the downward spout, through the lingering hiss,
through the other side all the way to China,
whose technology is growing evermore cooperative
than our paltry nanobots, until I kick back
in my own backyard where you then arrive
to find us throwing empty beer cans
at half-beaten shadows, wracking up the least
amount of dirty money in the neighborhood.
We get critical and spin some lazy beats
and ask ourselves to reproduce in the multimillions,
in the multiple seizures of real televisions,

until exhausted, lying unkempt on deathbeds,
we shoot across the backgrounds like
finally free wolves who forgive
our indiscretions against ourselves. As in,
Time: we just made that shit up.

—

Bio: *(Amy King')* **Of her most recent book, I Want to Make You Safe, John Ashbery described Amy King's poems as bringing "abstractions to brilliant, jagged life, emerging into rather than out of the busyness of living." King teaches English & Creative Writing at SUNY Nassau Community College and works with VIDA: Women in Literary Arts.**

Marilyn Kiss

Chilean Obituary: The Other September 11

For Pedro Pietri

A quiet reigns…
whispers, tiptoeing,
reverance…
A child lays
a rose at the base
of the marble slabs
Identities engraved in blood
rows and rows of them
reeking of tortures unnamable.

Disappeared.
Snatched from among us.
More than 3,000 of them.

Sobs escape from
blocked throats of grandmothers,
sisters, brothers, friends.

A generation is missing!

I stand with mourners,
the culpability of my passport
throbbing in my pocket
for before the planes and
the towers, before
the ash and the rubble,
long before there was
"nine eleven"

there were democratic elections and Popular Unity

There was Juan, a truck driver

There was Miguel, a worker in the Copper Mines
There was Milagros, a university student
There was Olga, a journalist
There was Manuel, a farmer
There was Salvador Allende, victorious,
in the Moneda Palace.

There was the Cold War
spreading fear in Washington
There was Nixon
There was Kissinger

There was the CIA

On the other September 11
there were helicopters
and coup-black limousines
There were tanks and artillery
and Allende
in his pathetic helmet

It was 1973.

Where were you?
Where was I?
Where was the horror when
Pinochet hijacked his nation
and butchered
Juan
Miguel
Milagros
Olga and
Manuel?

Juan, age 28
Miguel, age 33
Milagros, age 24
Olga, age 17
Manuel, age 19

Now in Chile
there is a monument
They can mention
these names,
restore to them their history
bemoan that
fateful September day
when terror overtook
the streets of Santiago
and Juan, Miguel,
Milagros, Olga,
Manuel, Cecilia,
Rosita, Carlos, Pablo, Luis, Margarita
Isabel, Jorge, Ramón, Cesár, Jesús
and their comrades began
to disappear
Forever.

Ron Kolm

The Summer They Killed The Spanish Poet

(After Philip Levine)

It's the end of summer.
My mother avoids the windows
Of our suburban house.
She opens her purse and
Checks the contents,
Looking for Kleenex amid the
Clutter to blot her tears
Because she's going
To visit the gypsies
Hoping they'll hook her up
With her dead husband.

She kisses me goodbye, taking
One last look in her purse.
I look, too, and am astonished
To see a tiny tableau inside–
A perfectly proportioned Garcia
Lorca about to meet his end
At the hands of a miniature
Firing squad (tho' how a kid
Like myself knows this, I'll
Never tell). My mother
Shuts her purse and leaves.

———

Bio: *(Ron Kolm)* Ron Kolm is a member of the Unbearables. He is a contributing editor of Sensitive Skin and the editor of the Evergreen Review. He is the author of The Plastic Factory and Divine Comedy (poems). Ron's papers were purchased by the New York University library, where they've been catalogued in the Fales Collection as part of the Downtown Writers Group.

Richard Kostelanetz

Within 'Richard Kostelanetz'

Centralized OK trash.
Stink crazed loather.
Slick not retard haze.
Dozen starchier talk.
Crazed trinkets halo.
Learnt this crazed OK.
The craziest, old rank.
At think loser crazed.
OK, cretin! Let's! hazard.
Crazed throats liken.
Zone rat slick hatred.
OK! this crazed rental.
Kinder zealot charts.
Crazed as hotter link.
Kinder zealots chart.
Crazed liars OK tenth.
Crazed or stale think.
Rant earth-sized lock.
Zealot hand trickers.
Loner dazes thick rat.
Thank crazed loser it.
Craziest held or tank.
Link crazes to hatred.
OK, halt! craziest nerd.

Crazed, loath stinker.
Daze rather slick not.
Centralized to shark.
Haze and slick rotter.
Tank craziest holder.
Hazel and to trickers.
Daze on trickers halt.
Drat! haze interlocks.
Christ! ranked zealot.
OK rant craziest held.
Haze or link detracts.
Daze interlock trash.
Crazed like not trash.
Daze scrotal thinker.
Darn! thicker zealots.
Crazed or in the talks.
Zero slick and the rat.
Earth-sized, torn lack.
Daze or the slick rant.
A crazed links hotter.
OK, let's, crazier hadn't.
Doze rather slick ant.
Slick rat haze rodent

Ptr Kozlowski

Coma Berenices / Pelo De Berenice / Berenice's Hair

A lot of these nights are like oceans full of rainstorms, windstorms,
straining for a port city - buildings and bedrooms - homes away from
home -
rocking here to this one and then again to that person,
you maybe cop a bright beacon beaming across the dance floor -
and teletype the touchtone to a voice from far away

swimming home through brain tissue trashed like a parking lot
Having sent two opposing navies
of molecules into my bloodstream
with one uncertain casualty and no unlikely winner

I just get these glimpses -
a couple of bright planets - or maybe it was Castor and Pollux -
appearing to be close out there through a narrow sight line
of a window and some buildings that are nearby;
her eyes through a smokescreen of bebopping shoulders,
her lips moving soundlessly to someone who is over there -
as the same variety of noises drowns out
most of what a voice near my ear is relating.

out on the uncrowded night highways, the traffic moves like schools
of fish -
glossing over hearthstones and overpassing paving bricks -
gravel at the seashore, gravel on the rooftops,
crushed glass popping under tires by the curbside -

Sometimes this hooking up routine is like an excuse to get through to
breakfast;
to awake in a new place and see what they've got hanging on the
walls,
and what you might see when you look out their window.

A way to find yourself out in the wee hours at the ocean beach -
looking for Berenice's Hair.
How the hell else are you ever going to get there?

Linda Lerner

Because It's A Dolphin

They stood for hours on the union street bridge
looking down at him struggling to get out of
the sewage filled Gowanus worst possible place
to get trapped in blocks from where I live and unaware
of what was happening till afterwards,
I told an old shoeshine man who'd come down from Harlem
with his supplies, moved to Breezy Point and taken up residence
outside this subway station after the storm;
"I saw the dolphin flail about, come up for air & fall
back down, and up again," a passerby said who'd overheard me.
one dollar a shine he called out to someone leaving the station
nodding as she spoke, "got stuck behind one of the pipes that
run along the sides of the canal, freed himself," *one dollar…*
"you should have seen it," she told us, "everyone was
taking photographs, routing for him each time
he came up …" was on the verge of tears and
he just kept nodding…. *one dollar one dollar a shine*
"so cold" she said, and no one could leave:
everyone was waiting for the tide to change

———

Bio: *(Linda Lerner)* Linda Lerner's Takes Guts & Years Sometimes was
published by NYQ books, 2011. She's previously published thirteen
collections of poetry. Forthcoming: a chapbook of poems inspired by
nursery rhymes illustrated by Donna Kerness (Lummox Press). Her next
full lenth collection, Yes, the Ducks Were Real, will by published by NYQ
books next year.

Tsaurah Litzky

Too Many

I want to find a better world, but everywhere I look
Shiva the Destroyer has been there before me,
filling the ash trays with chicken bones and crystal meth,
writing "I told you so" on mirrors with his rancid breath,
telling lies about poetry saying it is all sour grapes,
false advertising written by weirdos, losers, confusers and drunks,
everywhere I look I see too many black leather jackets,
too many sour pusses, too many long faces,
too many sentences beginning with "I",
too many bottles of blue-green Nyquil
downed in desperation at four in the morning,
too many spastics in wheelchairs maimed
in the preliminary squirmishes of desire
and every third one of them is me.
Some questions come up again and again.
why do some people feel their pain is greater, special,
worth more than my pain or your pain or the pain of the snail,
designed to move along a slimy path of its own secretions,
never to play basketball, never to fly?

Some questions come up again and again
Why do I keep breaking my knuckles trying to punch through iron
doors,
Why are the only Boddisattvas I meet liars and advertising whores,
Why, when I hook up with someone special new
I can't pass the tests he puts me through,
like going down on a Molotov cocktail,
or translating the Kama Sutra into Braille,
Why do I feel I have to earn love?
Isn't it everyone's right? Isn't it the only saving grace left?
Why are there more questions than answers,
Why is a doctor in China perfecting an acrylic womb,
Why can't I find any magic mushrooms?
Why is the ultimate pillow never on sale,

Why has Facebook become the unholy grail
Why is to manipulate to devour
Why has telling the truth fallen from power,
Why has the idea of free speech become such a bad girl,
Why have oysters lost their pearls?
Why are there too many black leather jackets in the world?

Veronica Liu

We Take A Few Minutes Before Clocking Out

"Come dance with me," you say, as you slink up the TV aisle. I
shimmy down Documentary and meet you by Staff Picks. We
sweep into a half-embrace, one set of arms protruding stiffly,
tango-style. Coasting by Anime, you say, "Gimme today's greatest
hits." I catalogue the shift with each pivot: "The computers crashed,
another dude quit, we've been told to emphasize Religion. We don't
understand the directive to 'Ban Karl Rove!'—language barrier?
bad joke? At lunch I realized it's been three years since I returned
Jacob's possessions after shrinkwrapping them in the storage
room. Then it began to pour rain so we all ordered Empire Corner."
Apologetic grins to the poor schmuck waiting to verify his credit card
at the unmanned desk before we twirl away toward Sci-fi. We dip and
lilt to an imaginary tune, a chimerical interlude against the backdrop
of cowboys shootin' 'em up onscreen.

Bio: *(Veronica Liu)* Veronica Liu's writing, comics, photography, and
silkscreen prints have been published in Broken Pencil, Quick Fiction,
Pax Americana, and other publications, and she has received artist grants
from Northern Manhattan Arts Alliance, Manhattan Community Arts Fund,
Citizens Committee, and the Goodman Fund. She is founder of Word
Up Community Bookshop, a volunteer-driven, multilingual, nonprofit
community space in Washington Heights.

Annmarie Lockhart

You Say Encyclopedia Britannica

but I hear *Chang and Eng.*

Entwined identical twin brothers
of Siamese descent, they were born
in China, escaped poverty via freak
show, became free agents, settled
in North Carolina (and here's where
it really gets weird), bought a plantation
and married a couple of local babes,
sisters, daughters of an itinerant minister.

Chang and Eng, newly naturalized,
had the *cojones* to buy slaves. No matter
how close to the bone, to their shared
liver, their own chains rattled, the only
freedom that interested them
pertained to commerce.

Between them (literally) they fathered
21 children in their custom-made
quadruple-sleeping bed. Imagine
the mechanics, the sheer kink
in a time of Puritan-tight stricture.
Consider the angles and dynamics,
the eternal un-privacy that pervaded
the world for two multiplied by two
then by ten and ten again.

Jump ahead to Y2K: At the sonogram
(not prescribed by law) the technician
delivers the news that I'm carrying twins
and I do not ask their gender or inquire
about the state of their health, but rather:
Are they conjoined?

Damn the Encyclopedia Britannica
for spitting out nothing memorable
beside this pair of sick SOBs whose
misfortunes, eccentricities, and failings
read straight out of reality TV. Chang
and Eng, the Siamese Twins, some
150-year-old hoax that would have
been outed on Snopes (dotcom)
had the internet been invented by
Mark Twain instead of Al Gore.

———

Bio: *(Annmarie Lockhart)* **Annmarie Lockhart is the founding editor of vox poetica, an online literary salon dedicated to bringing poetry into the everyday, and Unbound Content, an independent press for a boundless age. A lifelong resident of Bergen County, NJ, she lives, works, and writes two miles east of the hospital where she was born.**

Ellen Lytle

Summer And None

vermont afternoons swim slowly
mirror the bedroom window
in ralph's double-wide
pulling us under

july's breath

a drowning heat traps ralph
his crippled legs wheel
to the screen
no further

the animal sweat of lourie's farm
stunts hands on kitchen clocks

old combs, corroded forks,
moldy books skirted in grisly lint,
sinking into the good earth,
are now free

from rotten teeth
determined rain
and, on a day sun
scours the land

trees get pruned
grass mowed, paint and lumber
box the porches on east street, and
a pollarded tree in a front yard is safe

Sheila Maldonado

Great Blood

you come from greatness

remember that

you are the descendant of great kings

remember that

the descendant of great brutal kings

great big violent kings
who forced hundreds of slaves to make temples
still around to this day

you are from great big brutal kings
who tore out hearts
if they had to

who got big buildings made
that people who can afford it
still visit

remember that

if you have to
you can make people your slaves
and get your building up

you can tear out a heart

if you have to

you have kings in your blood

remember that

Stan Marcus

The Janitor Who Paints Oils
(Inspired by a painting by Palmer Hayden)

Under the lead pipes and the asbestos
the janitor who paints oils thinks the
physicality of the objects around him

are reducible to surfaces and the ideas
that have tickled him in the midst of the trash
are a summation of things he needs to express.

The inhaling of the building, the throbbing
he understands in the plaster, he has lived with
over the years, and not for a moment has he

distinguished them from the mice that scurry
under the crib of his son. The fragments of
the whole are endurable because he has named them

with pigments—not knowingly when he strokes
the canvas he can barely afford, but in his arm
is a language he has a notion of, as he stares

over the brush like man over a gun.
There is defiance in his renderings,
he is abandoned like the bottles he collects

each morning. Neither noon nor evening,
which he settles with a smile, but
under one bulb in the dank cellar,

the boiler, the broom icon, the beams sagging,
he is thrifty in his breathing as if the air
were parceled out between family and vermin.

The loud ticking of the abstract he never

hears in the mercy of his living and gives
no quarter to disturbances. No substance

is necessary for moving forward, but energy,
like fuses in the wires, he contains and
draws off for those dwelling above him.

Like a cat, he stretches out to the walls and sleeps.

Nancy Mercado

For The Charlatan Poet

> *How feeble our vocabulary in the face of death,*
> ---Billy Collins

Product of a frenzied empire; his last concubine

The disfigured wordsmith
Sells himself happily
Disguised as general of the people
A pencil for a gun
A degree for smoke and mirrors
A layer of black skin
For a cruel disguise

He gladly stalks stardom's tail
Reciting with fork tongue
Engaging the silly girls
The silly poets
With translucent lies, sights and sounds
A virtual circus

All the while
The planet hurls her anger
By land and sea
Convulses
Warping her dainty figure
To drive out corporate Beelzebubs
Polluted oil barons

Earth protects her wildlife

But this gluttonous fiend
This truly blind bastard; would be poet
Divides his time between
A wall mirror and a hand held mirror

Like Hitler
Is hypnotized
By his own conjured tongue

———

Bio: *(Nancy Mercado)* **Nancy Mercado is a board member and assistant editor for eco-poetry.org. Featured on National Public Radio's The Talk of the Nation and the PBS NewsHour Special: America Remembers 9/11, she has authored a poetry collection: It Concerns the Madness, 7 theater plays and edited if the world were mind: a children's' anthology. Her poetry and fiction have been extensively anthologized.**

Myrna Nieves

The Scream

The scream hurts in the core of my chest.
The scream suffocates.
Run.
The scream is on the verge of a precipice.
If it burst in silence,
The dawn will break into a thousand pieces.
But don't make a noise.
Yes, make a noise.
Scream.
Do not scream.
What are you going to do with the echo?
If you can't gather it, don't scream.
Ah, my chest.
My chest
My chest
Sheet of iron, lead
Heavy
Heavy
The scream is in the center cavity. Who has formed it?
Nobody wants to have a trapped scream.
But it is there.
There, there.
And in the temples.
Perhaps if you sleep
It would go to sleep
Or vanish like a cloud.
Ah, the scream.
Sleep.
Is it better than screaming?
There is no limit to the scream.
Long cord that has no ending.

Space rocket that does not leave the Earth
Or drags a heavy lump with it.
The scream awaits entangled.
It's an Exterminating Angel.

———

Bio: *(Myrna Nieves)* **Myrna Nieves is a writer, educator, editor and director for twenty years of the Boricua College Winter Poetry Series. Her books include: Libreta de sueños (narraciones), Viaje a la lluvia, poemas and Breaking Ground: Anthology of Puerto Rican Women Writers in New York 1980-2012. Nieves received the Literary Award (Fiction) of the PEN Club of Puerto Rico in 1998.**

Obsidian

Alfred

...and so i cried at
Alfred Washington's grave
there i heard piano keys
tickle ivories old jazz-time strokes
and Art Tatum was the most

Bible-thumping Alfred Washington
a cornucopia of useless historical biblical knowledge
and canonical tones

i was just a black boy
trapped in ghetto's plight broken
windows trying to escape his fate
black & white ivory keys
promised to set me free
from the chains of a forbidden
South Bronx rite

Alfred Washington was
Be-Bop's epitome of epic scale
chords and arpeggios
diatonic triads
"E G B D F
Every Good Boy Does Fine
G B D F E
F A C E
& A C E G"

Running my bony fingers up
and down the scales
became the new religion of
salvation to me
flat scales
sharps

and inversions
saved a nappy headed Negro
boy from gansta's delight
and dark foreboding jail cell's
cold steel blight

i quit my piano lessons
at 14 wanted to box and
play basketball
Sugar Ray Leonard
and Magic Johnson dreams
escape my father's screams
but i still hear Alfred Washington
tickling the ivories in between

finally i come to the
grave sight of a jazz musician
rhapsody's peaceful sleep
and bent my tired poet's
knees not to pray...
but to weep

Yuko Otomo

Water

I swallowed
a compelling amount of water
when I first learned to swim

since then
water strips the façade
of my fear to the core
whenever I face it

like any (il)logical irony
it melts me down
to the utmost comfort
when I am in it
& the ecstasy it provides
always seems like
it will last forever

in order to avoid
a startling splash on my face
I do not crawl on water
I float on it
although I have become
such an exceptionally good swimmer
over the years

I am 90% water
& had slept in it
for 9 months
before the moon pulled the tide

tonight
the moon is a pool of water
& I miss my parents & home

Eve Packer

What You Think

remember those parties,
those blue, or was it red, it was blue light parties
in someones queens basement
far from home, not on the D,
but some other train, trains,
all those bodies
close close teen bodies
somehow efrem george
inserts his knee
between yr legs
yr wearing a skirt
or dress. probably a skirt
and too tight sweater.
we didnt wear pants, jeans,
not at night
not to a blue light night party in queens
somehow he inserts his knee
now what
wanta look cool. what do i do
cant do the wriggle back.
cant move away. the only way to move
is closer
all those fun house mirror faces
the room spun honey
darling you send me, you know
you send me...honest you do...
that's sam cooke. i have a crush
on sam cooke. not his face.
i have no idea what he looks like.
his voice. those insinuations---
tenderness, caresse, something else
i dont quite get. not yet.
far from the bronx on the D
far from home

city blindfolded city
at peace, rest,
blindfolded city
night

wanna eat endless pizza
dream

Once upon a time the story you'll tell ozzy:
new melodies: 2009: songs, new beats in the air
and on the street

(you send me)

_____

Bio: *(Eve Packer)* **Eve Packer: bronx-born, poet/performer: 3 books
from fly by night press, most recent: new nails. 4 poetry/jazz CD's w/
saxophonist Noah Howard; 1 w/pianist/vocalist Stephanie Stone. lives
downtown, swims daily.**

Mireya Perez

When Abuelo Came To Visit

For Mario Bustillo Pareja

He wore a white linen suit
He changed twice a day
His panama hat with the black ribbon
A white ironed handkerchief at hand
As he came up the hill every afternoon at five
To visit his wife, Doña María

She had the bridge table ready and his cafecito
As she waited talcum-powdered, her hair in a bun
In her grey and white dress which softened
The black and white tiles of the veranda
The red hibiscus at the sides of the curving wide
Front steps in that corner house in the hills of El Prado
In that tropical city where I was born

The shade alcaparros with olive lace leaves
Kept watch in front as abuelito Mario
In his fresh white linen suit came up the hill
We all ran yelling "ahi viene abuelito"
Because we knew he had dulces for us
He had bought in la tienda de la esquina
Candies in small pieces of paper
Because there were no sealed cellophane bags
Enclosing candies
Dulces were loose then.

――――

Bio: *(Mireya Perez)* **My bilingual/bicultural background is an essential element in my choice of topics and modes of writing. I am a writer who brings two languages,Spanish and English, together to distill cultural meaning and sound. My work appears in Revista del Hada, Caribbean Review, Americas Review, Diosas en Bronce: Anthologhy of Colombian Women Writers, IRP Voices, among others.**

Puma Perl

Grace And Madness

Do you believe in grace and madness?
I am awed by motorcycles, scared of trucks
I can't shoot pool and I wish my face hadn't changed
Maybe it was my father's unexpected high-pitched laugh
or my mother's borderline ways
I rocked myself to sleep with dolls and cookies
Last night it was Romeo Void and sex toys
Never say Never.
I'd be lying if I said it really didn't matter
and I'm sorry I didn't take better care of you
Fear thrills me
Awe fills me
The blind dream in stereophonic sound
and we were all under water
Waiting for grace
Living in madness
Sometimes I can't believe that I breathe.

Su Polo

Apartment

There is a wind that is filled with the scent of the sea;
Freshness for a musty apartment.
Occasionally, in the airshaft between buildings,
The sound of a crow cawing, cawing, cawing –
Echoes as if from far off.
Then the smell of shampoo and sound of the shower.
Who is singing? I don't know.
Hairdryer and various alarms. Wake up – go to work.
Get going all of us.
Music – muffled by windows and curtains.
A baby is crying.
Lullabye.

Jim Porter

Untitled

The skimming of the water
Makes my bread moldy,
And up strikes the bell from faltering eyes.

The milky skin that soothes the mushroom,
Sows my green tea
And steals the life from out the sighs.

The mold that lies within the sighs,
Drifts like germs within a lake
And looms its cloud at the net.

The mold that sighs within the lies,
Cannot sing without the lark
That strings its sound through the skies.

The sigh that molds,
Clouds and breathes with
Sensual inklings of the cell.

"Subdue the urge that grasps for force,
For force will only lock wet sand."

Joy flows toward the sought, split cell,
Toward more gentle, wider sucking.

"And if the yeast be only wine;
Still, make my bread moldy."

———

Bio: *(Jim Porter)* **Jim Porter says: "ALL MY POEMS SUCK," and having
said that; they are "SURREAL VISIONS OF DELIGHT WITH A MIXTURE OF
COSMIC TOM-FOOLERY, PSYCHIC TREMORS, GENTLY BUFFOONERY,
SHEER LOVE AND MAGICAL SCENES FROM NATURE."**

John Marcus Powell

The Bottom Of Christopher Street

At the bottom, Christopher Street meets a highway.
On the other side is the Hudson. The flow is undetectable. It ain't
going nowhere.
Journey near complete. I cross over and walk out onto the pier. In
the seventies
this pier was ready to fall into the water, it was so decayed.
This was the area for Homo Roaming.
Nobody asked ' will you marry me? as the pier collapsed into the
river
as we let our bodies have their sway.
This new pier has rails not walls so is open to all elements.
It's a meeting place for Teeny- Pervs, for Hurly-girlies
Whose parents have chucked them to the wolves that swarm the
democratic streets

A few miles down is Lucy Liberty, the famed cross-dresser.
who stands where the river is neither bay nor river, the bay not yet a
bay.
Her real name's Larry.
This is revealed when she turns towards New Jersey. Nightly, on the
sly.
With her back turned towards us, she is on the look-out for
foreigners.
Instead of acquiescence
she blares a question not based on the American or any kind of
dream.

Lucy wants to know "WHAT'S THE NAME OF THIS WATER."
"Strip of water,' comes an uneducated reply.
A more educated voice proffers, "This is the estuary meeting the
Atlantic."
Lucy Liberty instructs, "WHEN I ASK A QUESTION I PROVIDE THE
ANSWER.
I'M THE ONLY ONE PRESENT NOT INCLINED TO
OVERPONDER."
She opens her lips and sexily hisses:
                              "SEA"

Ron Price

Circling San Michelle

approaching Pound's grave

One hawk and a quick spit of land
surrounded by water. Around this boat
there is only water
and other boats circling the island –
and one bound with the dead
making a straight, a solemn line
through rain
toward the island sinking
in the alluvial muck and dreck
it rose out of –
the island, the boatmen, all of us.
How difficult to grasp
the world, hard to handle it, know it.
There is such work to be done,
good work
distinguishing silt from the sand
water deposits – for the past is food.
What thou lovest well remains
to nourish or corrupt.
Knowst'ou wing from tail?
All afternoon circling this island,
one hawk and a quick spit of land
divided by water
from the work, not the danger,
always the danger of
getting lost, going down.
All day feeling time, the falling rain.

JD Rage

The Darkness

My dreams are getting darker
I'm worried about the Hellhound
I should have gotten some tattoos of
The River Styx

The river monster vanished
before my eyes and in his place
appeared rushing waters full of
bigger monsters and ravenous wolves
swimming in the Styx and the boatman
waiting—waiting—

I surprised the surrounding family
by jumping across the mist, then reappearing
wrapped in the Grim Reaper's cloak

I smiled and my jaw fell off
I had turned into a toothless skeleton
I couldn't walk, so I had to fly
The wolves howling—howling--
I howled too and they tucked their tails
to skulk away

Then, having no choice,
I turned around and headed
back into the dust

Vittoria repetto

At Columbus Park

after i finish feeding them,

the sparrows watch me,

perch on the bench besides me

hoping for more.

one or two play chicken with me

flying so close to my head

i feel the half second breeze of their wings.

———

Bio: *(Vittoria repetto)* **Vittoria repetto's poetry book Not Just A Personal Ad published by Guernica Editions highlights the voice of a distinctly working class, distinctly lesbian, and distinctly Italian American poet from downtown Manhattan who maintains an ear for both the actual language of daily life and literary echoes. She has been hosting the Women's/Trans' Poetry Jam at Bluestockings Bookstore since 1999.**

Yolanda Rodriguez

Foolish Heart

Foolish heart that tries again
To follow an irreverent path towards happiness!

At the beginning:
My tangled, thickened blood stirs
itself to let my heart beat
In his sad home.
My curves will sway once more
and my broken wings will open.
The intoxicating fragrance of mayhem
will place itself in my mouth.
My feelings shall be as clear as the river waters
Uncertainty will whisper in my ear once again
to play with the obstacle of my reasoning.

The Result:
My being will be scattered in his warm dissolving breath.
The sanity will be gone when the novelty
of his mind is whispered to me.
The vision of my senses will darken
and I will faint at his touch.
As his pain is revealed
the ground beneath my feet will diminish.
His cutting history will empty my insides and take over.
My sorrows will drown in themselves.
I will want the light of his eyes without the thunder
and lightning…only their soft glow.
I will only want the rain on his back
to break with its weight the fossilized stone in my chest... (pulverizing it).

How do you love again?
How does one put restrains on desire?
Without opening the river of deception…
Without closing the sky…

———

Bio: *(Yolanda Luz Rodriguez)* Yolanda Luz Rodriguez is the Co-Founder of Visiones Culturales (www.visionesculturales.com) and writes poetry since 1997. In 2011 she began to publish her work in her blog www.thesoundsofmialma.com. Recently, she self-published her first poetry book titled Alma Derramada/Spilled Soul which is a handmade book made by Yarisa Colon. She writes in both English and Spanish.

Robert Roth

Charisma

I saw my mother in the hospital yesterday. A visitor came by. Someone whom she has spoken to for years on the phone. Ruth, a woman younger than myself, the daughter of a friend of my mother's who had a four year ending badly painful affair with a psychoanalyst, a "brilliant charismatic" man who touched her in deep and profound places. Places, she said that her husband could never reach. At the time she told her husband straight out about what was happening; he still wanted to be with her but she told him that she had to leave him. After her break up with the psychoanalyst she returned to her husband. From time to time, she still sees the ex-lover who has grown very old and frail, and helps take care of him.

My mother suddenly very alert waded headlong into the conversation, constantly referring to the ex-lover as "That son of a bitch." In truth her words seemed to grow more out of loyalty than real conviction. But when Ruth insisted that she wasn't a passive victim in the affair, that it was something that she chose to do, my mother answered that charisma was a powerful allure and people with it have some responsibility for its power. Back and forth. Great discussion about love, life and desire.

Marvin W. Schwartz
What does the motive matter.

Thaddeus Rutkowski

The Truth About The Tooth Fairy

"I know you're the tooth fairy," she says to me. She picks up the dollar coin left under her pillow. "It's change from your MetroCard!"

She means the MetroCard machine, where I bought a subway pass earlier in the day and received a silver dollar in my change.

My concern was that I hadn't left her enough money, that a dollar wasn't enough for a lost molar. I didn't think I'd be exposed for who I was (a daily subway rider) and who I was not (the tooth fairy).

Without my powers, will I be able to convince her, when her sock is filled at Christmas, that Santa has visited? For that matter, when Halloween rolls around, will the jack o' lantern—complete with glowing leer—lose its frightening aspect? During Hanukkah, will the candles of the Maccabees fail to remind her of the one-day oil that burned for eight days? And in the spring, will the Easter bowl of colored eggs fail to summon the bunny?

No doubt these sleights of mind won't go over anymore. But the spirit will remain. We'll tack up the socks, carve the pumpkin, light the candles and paint the eggs. We'll even leave a contribution from the tooth fairy, though not in MetroCard change. We'll channel the magic that we don't understand with the primitive tools we have.

———

Bio: *(Thaddeus Rutkowski)* Thaddeus Rutkowski is the author of the novels Haywire, Tetched and Roughhouse. All three books were finalists for an Asian American Literary Award, and Haywire won the Members' Choice Award. He received a 2012 fiction writing fellowship from the New York Foundation for the Arts.

Annie Sauter

Liar

In an attic in a house on Pardee Street
I want to be floating
Riding on the thigh
Of an idea that
   Can never be made
   Into clarity.

I want to feel the word
-Made flesh of you,
   But with amnesiac fingers.
   Then spend, forgettable hours
On featureless streets.

Late at night,
I want a bar-room tamale, wrapped In corn sheaves,
   tight like the red-string
   I tied to my ring
Finger, to
Remind me. That I want it.

At the midnight-liquor store. The man,
   Hot as rancid foil, grease-fine from behind
   The counter digs deep, into that ethereal Jar,
To bring it up,
Rings it up with my wake-Up.

Somewhere
Near the corner of Ashby and
Grove, I finish them both off.

Before passing out
"Baby"
You say,
"Let me".
   I untie the string

Ilka Scobie

Invocation

Think about something other then your career (or lack thereof)
your romance, your health, your finances, your past and your future
Observe and empathize with another sentient being
Nurture your body - anyway you can
Expand your mind, except with superstitions
Give up one vice
or cultivate another, which you will drop as soon as possible
Walk more, either on concrete, or preferably earth
Get a land line and unplug your devices for one entire day
Help someone; it can be easy as listening or carrying a grocery bag
Contemplate a mercy fuck, the benefits might surprise you
Seek community for sustenance
From morning to night, consume no food that is white

Susan Scutti

Subtraction

A part of you is unborn
a slender fold within your mother's womb
where you remain hidden from anger and ambition and
meanwhile most of you lives
a blameless existence in a city where
distortion is a general tendency.

And so you listen to the notes of resolution
going flat or sharp unexpectedly.

Last night a man accepted your dollar bills ---
unclean and crumpled like used and discarded tissues ---
and then he stared with dark eyes
as you spoke a guttural language of neglect.

After returning to your pillbox apartment
you imagined him asleep and folded between sheets
floating on a weary silence
each night as your mother does.

———

And So The Train To Brooklyn

The heft of private grief
Bends the posture of this shuffling crowd:
Sap within a rootless tree.

Susan Sherman

The Death Of A Thousand Cuts

No one blow alone is lethal   The poison builds slowly
healing seductive   promising release   only to be opened
at another time   another place   *Ling Chi*   the death
of a thousand cuts   Torture reserved for the vilest of deeds
or for the rebel   the one who doesn't fit   The ultimate warning
where not to entrust the heart   *Ling Chi*   in modern parlance
creeping normality   unacceptable propositions occurring
in small unnoticeable increments   until damage is irrevocable
Ice melting into water   filling the vastness of an ocean
dissolving from below   Chunks crack   and fall
a shock wave   the obscene myth of vanquishing grief
Denial anger forgiveness acceptance   As islands are
swallowed up   populations displaced   *Live somewhere else*
leave what you love   move on   As if love were a subway stop
as if you were holding up a restless queue
when what is dear to you is sliced away   First a finger
then an arm   a leg   the heart   *Ling Chi*   the scar remains
a network of twisted veins   The soul bleeds red
How long before the point of no return is reached

———

Bio: *(Susan Sherman)* **Susan Sherman: Most recent books are America's
Child: a woman's journey through the radical Sixties (Curbstone/
Northwestern University Press, 2007); The Light that Puts an End to
Dreams: New and Selected Poems (Wings Press, 2012); Nirvana on Ninth
Street : Short Fiction (Wings Press, publication date Fall, 2014)**

Larissa Shmailo

Over

On the perfect roof, near a perfect ledge,
A small terra firma with a narrow edge,
No temporizing with last-minute balance,
No handhold, no foothold, no anchor, no ballast.
And once committed, once into the air,
No hovering, no kiting, no waiting there.
The polygonal street and the shining dark cars
Attacked at meters per second squared.
Once over, soon over: a thing done just once:
Like fireworks and New Years' bells, fast and intense,
Quite finite, soon finished, thought long, slow begun,
And forgotten by others like the old year now done.

Danny Shot

Mo's Bar April, Fort Greene

Vaginas and Crucifixes and Blood
says Tim, that's what I want in a poem
big V, bic C, big B.
Nobody can disagree as we stand
on the corner of DeKalb and South Portland
sucking on cigarettes weighing the implications…

and so begins the weekend.
Miguel Algarin inside the bar, drunk
ready to have a serious conversation
about the trouble with women.

Robin tells us of Elizabeth Bishop
and Lola in Brazil, of infidelity
and suicide and moving on.
Adam speaks of a Sea World
water slide past dolphins
at 60 miles an hour.

Never-ending winter over,
today's the day where everything
pops and Brooklyn's blooming
green, bud-luscious.
Welcome to the spring
Mr. Pollyanna. L'chaim
Have another drink.

Earlier today Emilie showed me
a book about reading eyes,
said it reminds her of when I stop
walking, deep in thought,
it provides a key to what
might be in my mind

though I know the truth:
sometimes I just stop
to let the world spin
as I take it in and marvel
at the wonder of it all.

Robert Siek

Bang Bang Behind An Aquarium

He asked her if it was just bang bang,
sitting behind me on a NJ Transit train.
I guess that's not dating a mutual friend
but sex here and there, needs filled,
fucking on a couch in a furnished basement,
the unprotected splitting halves on cushions,
wet opening battered, a marsupial pouch fisted
behind a fifty-gallon aquarium, football trophies
on shelves built into walls, displayed since childhood,
his baby arm pounding a drum, lodged pink deep,
a diaphragm for birth control but she's on the pill.
It's just his hips against her bottom: bang bang
they say, like gun shots in the Outback,
kangaroos wiping out face first,
buckshot in hides, wet spots,
stains on upholstery. He doesn't ask
how often this happens, but says do what
you want to do. Three more stops and I'm out
of here. Music not loud enough played from an iPod,
a new term overheard, and it's not yet St. Patrick's Day,
the parade happening, couches waiting for company,
all floors in houses or apartments outside of the city,
dinner at Outback, rare steak and lobster tail,
no salad, the pink inside bleeding on a plate,
something pulled limp from a pouch, dead joey.
Bang bang he said. Her legs still spread.
She's leaking an aquarium of hungry fish.

Fred Simpson

No Poem Here

"Ice cold wahta he-uh, one dolla.
Got a buck, you're in luck", said the vendor with a cooler.
But no luck for me. No poem here.
Just the beach.

And the most pregnant woman I've ever seen.
Gotta be due yesterday,
belly protruding straight out;
perfect beach ball she carries sits up high.
Portends a boy, I'm told.
New life any day
but no poem.

To my left a redhead turns strawberry blond
right before my eyes.
Kudos to the sun.
Different kind of hot where waves lap sand.
Can take the heat much longer, no shade;
just sun tan lotion and swim trunks on;
no office cubicles, no car horns.

Thank God no loud radios -- my preference is for silence.
Everything in balance except for one bore piercing the mix;
his inflections like there's no other way/
what he says, take verbatim/ no doubt/ he is sure!
Mercifully his voice just peppers now and then.
Maybe soon he'll go home.
Still, there is no poem.

Just this therapeutic, synthesized milieu:
tan sand, blue-green ocean, hazy horizon at two p.m.,
jutting rocks, the distant pier, no socks....

"Ice cold wahta he-uh, one dolla.

Got a buck, you're in luck", said the vendor with a cooler.
But no luck for me. No poem here.
Just the beach.

———

Bio: *(Fred Simpson)* **Poems in Mobius, The Poetry Magazine's 29th &
30th Eds. & Riverside Poets Workshop, Vol.13.; featured for various series
including Green Pavilion, Saturn Series & Ken Siegelman's Brooklyn Poetry
Outreach at B&N. I enjoy accompanying my readings by playing the drum.
Current project: my Sunrise Series of Poetry.**

Joanna Sit

Butter For Use

People often laugh at my comic stories
of poverty in the squatters' village,
as refugee and illegal immigrant before
I was nine. Mostly, though, they're nostalgic for

me, for the long way I've come, as if I were
a runner who'd tripped at the start but came in
second. I can see the image they've cooked
up, romantic and satisfying to see me

at their table, on their lawn, by the seaside
in the sunset, tan and healthy. At last.
Like a feel-good movie. Like a beacon of hope.
To hammer in Ragged Dick's cliché, I throw in

details of tropical misery – tuberculosis and intestinal
worms from chewed and spitted sugar canes, insects
in the apple, tin roof over mud floor,
colonial cruelty and municipal alms.

But away from the rapt audience, when I return
to myself, when I'm alone, I'm never hungry
for those days of waiting in line

every week for that government butter,
useless tubs of British charity I hauled
back for my family to sit on while we strung up

pearl necklaces, copper beads between tin seeds,
plastic bouquets, each leaf crowned by lime green fern
in our public housing, our one room life.

Although we steamed with water and fried with oil,
I collected the vats all the Tuesdays and stacked them up,

stood on them to reach for rice or climb to bed
and that was what butter looked like, what it was used for

until age thirteen I got into Avenue U Theatre's 70 cents
Wednesday double-feature of *Carnal Knowledge*
and *Last Tango in Paris,* when Marlon Brando
by then hysterical and numbed by want,

besieged by riddles of the rose and rage
directed Marie Schneider how to cut
her nail and use that stick of butter

so he might cross over that abyss of disgrace
to feed on the finger of retribution.
Maybe like him, it's too late and I'm too far

gone to accept the better moment
without dragging in the shame, to forget
what we were like once or take to heart

the plenty manifest: Cote du Rhone,
Champagne cocktail, steak au poivre,
quiche Lorraine, rosemary infused olive
oil in which to dip the artisanal loaf.

Unlike him though, I recognize
the moment when it's enough
deliverance to stand by myself

in a quiet morning, in an empty kitchen
and spread the butter on toast
like everyone else.

George Spencer

Guys With Guns And Profiles

2 black cops come to check
a suspicious
white guy
at the country club
He's armed with
a driver a 5 iron a mashy a putter
Starts to pull something out of his golf bag
Hard to see white guys in the bright sun
Cops fired 100 bullets
Fifty from each gun
Investigation
Exoneration

Diane Spodarek

Lose The Day (The Rose Bordello Song)

Lose the day
Lose the night
Lose the day and you lose your need to fight
        To always be right/to always be right

Five forty pm train
This is the second night he's acting strange
        I think he's high

Oh baby I miss you
I was so into you I gave up our daughter
Now she's a dancer some where on Vivian Street
Dancing for all your friends

Oh baby don't get drunk and go down to the Rose Bordello
You just might make the mistake of sleeping with our daughter
She doesn't look anything like you
        Or me
She's beautiful

Lose the day and lose the night
Lose the day and you lose your need to fight
to always be right/to always be right

Lose the Day
Lose the Night

––––

Bio: *(Diane Spodarek)* Diane Spodarek is an award winning Canadian-American artist, writer, playwright, poet, and a recipient of artist's fellowships from the NEA and NYFA. Publication in "KGB Lit Magazine," "Young Women's Monologues from Contemporary Plays," and forthcoming in "Ultra Short Memoir." She was the "runner-up" in the first Grand Poetry Slam at the Nuoyrican Poets Café in 1990. She's working on new songs for The Dangerous Diane Band in Detroit and lives in NYC.

Miriam Stanley

Always

There are scratches on the walls of the gas chamber.
Claw marks made by the gasping, trying to dig their way out.
Almost a graffiti obscene to visitors.
The hands, the nails, digging into own throats, dry and hot as ovens.

And today children gasp for air.

They are on the floor, fish flopping on the beach of battle, wide-eyed, brown irises with
dilated pupils.

They claw the air, grasp for dead mothers, or angels, or the doctors that crouch over them with
oxygen masks.

These children are Arab, Syrian, probably Muslim, does it matter?

My relatives clench the hems of my mind, their corpses alive in my dreams. These
relatives also gassed. Grey...stiff... bloated.

I go on the internet. Email my senators. Type in uppercase : WE HAVE TO DO SOMETHING...
I never hear back. Words fall into a dark space filled with bodies.

―――

Bio: *(Miriam Stanley)* Miriam Stanley is a Capricorn who floats in a sea of self-pity. She also loves to write.

Elizabeth Akin Stelling

Can't Shake These Old Cowgirl Blues

While writing in solitude in Newark, NJ

My peace has been disturbed
by bandits talking loudly outside
in the street, maybe it's the hallway.
They are flushing out my dreams—
almost highway robbery.

I believe they are extremely
older and deafer than my husband.
Going in and out
letting the door slam behind them.
I'll rush in
blind them with flashy charm,

and my six shooter smile.
Always loaded for prosperity.
After polishing up my tin star
since I can't shake them
no how,
here we go without spurs,

and that dagnabbit sun
hasn't even peered out
over the buildings or
through my sixth floor window.
A downtown hiatus gone awry
way way way north of the Pecos.

———

Bio: *(Elizabeth Akin Stelling)* Hailing from Texas, transplanted to New
Jersey by way of St. Louis, Elizabeth Akin Stelling is a force of nature.
She is a wife, mother, chef, a writer, an activist, and insomniac. Elizabeth

is managing editor of Z-composition Magazine, and has works published in vox poetica, Referential Magazine, getSpark, NJMonthly, Wild River Review, River Poets Quarterly, RePrint, Tuck Magazine, Linden Avenue Lit, Wordgathering, US1 Summer Fiction, and trade magazine- BizN4NJ. Her food poetry has been heard on CroptoCuisine Radio. Elizabeth's first full length poetry book is forthcoming in January, 2014- My South By Southwest Cast Iron Tempo Recollection, poetry and prose by Red Dashboard LLC Publishing; it reflects her growing up in the vastness of a Lone Star mindset.

Alice B. Talkless

The Emperor Of Health

As he got on top of her he felt at last truly in place, conqueror of this
kingdom of things. Manfully he bit his lip. Now his breath was
turbulent – an ordeal,
but he'd been touched that she'd gone to the trouble of a faked
orgasm.
That's the kind of sex she liked; dead and fake so the sense of
tranquility
cannot wholly persist. Then he had another and another, all of them
the same in their dismal contours.

He stepped back and fished in his pocket to produce a transmitter
and set it on the windowsill.

"I am less interested in the aesthetics of the ordinary
than participating in the fight for the ordinary."
"I don't want to get into a political discussion. Let's
just talk about you and how you react to all of this."
The ordinary is always contested ground.

PART 2
I guess it was yesterday, no maybe today there were four of us
waiting to go
to the free clinic for antibiotics and Kwell. The cracked old concrete
was slippery
with sweat, impetigo, athlete's foot, stroke, paralysis, labarynthine
vertigo, aphasia, insanity. Death has ten thousand several doorways.

PART 3
A lot of domestic things get shouted in public and so when I am
buying those socks and the mom in line behind me shouts "I Love
You" into her little phone –
I am powerless not to feel something is being performed – over-
performed – publicly performed, defiantly inflicted.
The ordinary is always contested ground.

PART 4

We hauled in big industrial guns, called it a solution and then we lied. "Dear Savages, forgive us but we need all our guns for ourselves. Next time we will bring some for you – yes, unless mischance occurs."

Mary Jane Tenerelli

Day 7: The Woods

The woods behind the hospital
Are vast
And ugly in the November light,
Old horse dung and
Low lying scrub,
And quiet
Like somebody holding their breath.
The person who told me
You were here
Has got to be wrong.
Your clothes are too light
And you forgot your winter coat.
I call your name
In a half-hearted way, frightened
Of what might come out of the trees.
I am too old for this
I think, and
Please don't let him spend
The night here,
Adding to my list
Of favors from God.
Then I go back to the car.
Maybe you're in
The McDonald's parking lot.
Maybe you are asleep
On the living room couch.
You are not here.
Please God, you are not here.

Zev Torres

Slow Fade Into Shock

Nothing was there
Other than a boldfaced title
Italicized letters
Followed by blank space
A page full of emptiness
Suggesting loneliness
A void
A cipher
Neglected and forgotten
Unattended and deprived.

Perhaps to be spared the fate
Of so many other pieces of paper
Scribbled upon
Then crumpled into a ball and tossed
Into the fire
Or more likely a waste paper basket
Lined with a plastic bag
Denied the opportunity to be recycled
To rise up and live again
To realize its potential.

Charlie Vazquez

Huracán Express

The bandit train glides into the night
Just as the storm arrives, just before sunrise
On its snake train journey through night's valley
It barrels toward the darkness of the Mare Orientale
A centipede mambo toward the netherworld
Crawling toward where no soul dares to go
It tracks the horizon's spine, this phantom sublime
On its zigzag swansong runaway line
Mortals stampede as it races toward the arms of the storm
As the sidewinder spine-twisting headwinds swarm
Heed your creed as their dizzying speed
Will cause this abandoned city to bleed
There's no escaping the fangs of the storm
Once this eve of damnation's morning is born
It heaves like thieves and hurls rain like knives
From its dark domain of the exploding sky
And by its furious and swelling seas
We'll be brought to our knees
We slither in and out of alien skin
And watch as new and impossible life begins
As this suicide ghost train flies on its forever ride
To the heart of the storm…
Though to get through alive
You'll need to ride it inside

Bio: *(Charlie Vázquez)* Bronx-based Charlie Vázquez is the author of
the novels Buzz and Israel and Contraband, as well as the bilingual poetry
collection Meditations: Bronx/Salsa. He co-authored the erotic poetry
collection Hustler Rave XXX with San Juan-based writer and translator
David Caleb Acevedo in 2013, and is writing a collection of Puerto Rican
ghost/horror stories.

Alfredo Villanueva-Collado

From Beast Meditates On Beauty

(1)
Sometimes, when
Beauty gets too close
and smiles, and you can
feel the flutter in
your stomach, look
the other way, curse
the day you were given eyes.

(2)
A beautiful friend I wear
in public, at crowded
affairs, as a way of affirming
Beauty has opted for me
to share its
epiphany.

(12)
Beauty is
the most insidious
disease in the books.

Beautiful ones
infect by their being.

They cannot die
from images in mirrors.

We die, believing
life is nothing without them.

(13)
Because I wanted many more than would have me
and some laughed at my propositioning

and others I did not dare approach,
I stole from each its most prized feature
--long eyelashes, small ears, round behinds--
and set it up on a shelf in a room

where empty-gazed I lick my wounds
wanting the whole of which I have a part.
I am called a poet, and a collector.

George Wallace

Warhol Soup

hey waiter waiter what's this jellyfish doing in my Warhol soup -- why I'll tell you mister it's doing the watusi it's doing the backstroke it's doing the merengue & the fly

it's meditating like a fuck bunny from mars it's a devil in disguise & it'll screw you up with its silkscreen elvis & its angular ass & tits with its wingtips & its long sharp teeth

but waiter waiter what's this marilyn doing in my Warhol soup -- why you don't know what you're messing with mister it's doing the 'i tease you' it's doing the 'turn me on dead man'

it's doing the i use you, you use me -- the i suck you, i eat you, then i spit you out like snake meat on a cold plate routine

but waiter waiter what's this mushroom cloud doing in my Warhol soup -- why listen up mister it's doing the edie it's doing the joe

it's doing the heroin freak the hedonist rag it's doing the candy darling the nico the ultraviolet & the lou reed too -- & if i told you once i told you a thousand times

a spoonful of that long hard darkness will get you all tangled up & wishing you could throw that bitches broth away but you can't

———

Bio: *(George Wallace)* **George Wallace is Writer in Residence at the Walt Whitman Birthplace, first poet laureate of Suffolk County NY, and author of 26 chapbooks of poetry, including Poppin Johnny (Three Rooms Press, NYC '10), Burn My Heart in Wet Sand (Troubador Press, Leicester UK, '05) and Swimming Through Water (La-Finestra Editrice, Trento, It, '05). An adjunct professor with the English Department at Pace University in Manhattan, he is editor of Poetrybay, Poetryvlog, Walt's Corner, and co-editor of Great Weather For Media and Long Island Quarterly.**

Bruce Weber

What Is That Strange Humming?

what is that strange humming? is it a horde of moscitoes circling its
prey in the dark house across the way? is it the voice of a young girl
oozing soap across the landscape of her skin? is it the refrigerator
greeting a fresh gust of electricity seeping into its chilly bones?
could it be coming from the hollow of the bark of that maple tree
bending like a horse to drink from the pool of water along the road?
could it be emanating from that halo on the head of st. sebastian in
the scene of martyrdom from the period of the black plague? is it
echoing in the memory of that old crone hobbling across the street
to perch at the door of the cathedral with a cup and a plea? maybe
its coming from behind the closed door of the maids in the attic
or from the squirrels maneuvering acorns into the earth or maybe
it's merely a shadow lingering in the full figure of an illusion or a
preposterous trick played by an imposter lurking in the back roads of
the mind holding a puppeteer's strings or maybe it's a void empty of
sound bereft of hello's where all things dwindle to zero escaping into
air like breath or electrons or the dust at the end of a long trail toward
god and salvation and the cure for all things great and small

———

Bio: *(Bruce Weber)* Bruce Weber is the founder and principle organizer of
the Alternative New Year's Day Spoken Word / Performance Extravaganza.

Estha Weiner

New Year's Eve

I choose to kiss no one, as the clock

turns to the next chance for all

of us who used to raise a glass

more easily to everything,

including life, and now know just

enough to toast to the possibility

of good champagne we can afford,

and leave the dreams

to the silence and the shriek

of our own respective, fragile sleeps.

(*From "Transfiguration Begins At Home", Tiger Bark Press, 2009)

――――

Bio: *(Estha Weiner)* Estha Weiner is co-editor and contributor to Blues For Bill: A Tribute To William Matthews (Akron Poetry Series, 2005) and author of The Mistress Manuscript (Book Works, 2009), Transfiguration Begins At Home (Tiger Bark Press, 2009),and. In the Weather of the World (Salmon Poetry, Ireland, 2013), She was a 2005 winner of a Paterson Poetry Prize, and 2008 Visiting Scholar at The Shakespeare Institute.

Colleen Whitaker

Miss Pontiac

Hot asphalt and ribbons of steel
Sunday crowds roar surrounds Me surreal
Motion cuts through the air
rumbles the ground beneath Me
His presence there
bold, victorious
and I become a piece of history

Platinum blonde and satin ribbon on My chest
says Miss Pontiac looks better then the rest
Pink and white floral
strike My femme fatale style
clashes with gold and black machines
Reflections of a moment in the light
With him there on this night

Flash & Danger lingers vivid
in My intense release
Spikes sink in to score My stance
anchor Me to a second glance
Perfect pose, perfect smile
Flash go the cameras

Trophy in My gloved hand feels just right
Mirror gloss and glitter
through the grease smeared night
He's tall and lean beside Me
Sweat running down his brow
The one in the winners circle
Clink flash go the cameras

Pose and smile, he's in the center
But through the lens they focus on Me
He's going down in history
and they all look at Me
Miss Pontiac looks better than all the rest
I'm all they're going to see

134

Francine Witte

Derby

Forget what you hear, every horse
is the same, lined up and waiting,
standing still at the same speed.
But when the starting gun cracks
its cold command across the back
of a Kentucky afternoon, there's a hush
in the air, and the crowd lifts out
of their seats, and briefly, their lives.
And it's like that second that love stops
winking her shadowed eye, so you finally move
to close in, when whatever you bet on
a minute ago has faded from the sheets
where you thought you had circled a winner,
and the track was tested and sure. But, listen,
a favorite is only a good-looking plug
who's been beating the odds until now.
Just lift up the gate, and his ankle could twist.
like a question, in the mud. Or take off his blinkers,
spook him with the hooves of the horse next door
and he's running the other way. A turn
of the weather, the wrong batch of oats
could throw a wall of air in front
of anything, a lover's heart, or the nose
of a horse whose neck is stretched across
the finish line, where the sun has shifted left,
his own shadow coming in first.

——

Bio: *(Francine Witte)* Francine Witte is a poet and fiction writer. Her poetry chapbooks are "First Rain" and "Only, Not Only." Her flash fiction chapbooks are "The Wind Twirls Everything" and "Cold June." She lives in Manhattan and is an English teacher.

Liza Wolsky

Package

You are a package tied with string
you are the german-425 steel knife I use to cut it open.

You are an unopened menu,
with a little bit of banana creme on one of its
lower
corners.

Jeffrey Cyphers Wright

Mind Your Business

> *"The astronauts were weeping"*
> David Shapiro

Together we've singed night's black wing.
Together we've wrecked the train.
Too many of us blue drag —
smokestack hurricanes. Futile
fuses for the few, poets shovel
love letters into furnaces unresigned.
Keep the motor running, hotfoot.
SKIPPING OVER DAMAGED SECTION
All the hubbub will you nothing buy.
Hubba hubba!
Steal the light, mug the sun.
Let dragons lick your burning tears.
Stop global warming, Camp Fire girl.
That's your job now, what you're here for.

Susan Yung

Work

"WORK" has always been a problem for me ever since I always had a fear that I'm not qualified to do the job due to my Asian descent esp. in the arts. I have recently watched "Mad Men" of the advertising business in the 60s and in the first episode only one brief scene of a Chinese family eating in an advertiser's office after he returned from vacation. It was a funny "racist" joke. A prelude image to the Vietnam War that Asians were uncivilized and needed to be revivified after we started the paper money system, looked sexy in cheongsam garments, learned to wash, starch their clothes, and worked on the RR building tunnels through the Rocky Mts.

All due respect, I have worked in the fields of Oregon picking strawberries, raspberries, waxed yellow & green beans. At the age of 8 I got my social security # before anybody in my peer group.

Many years later, in 1984, I went to the Philippines for an Oxfam study tour to Cebu where I turned a corner and quickly snapped this photo. She is probably weaving baskets to be sold in NYC's Bloomingdales. I doubt she ever got paid minimum wages.

As for myself, I had worked as a freelance typesetter for 25 years until everyone had computers and could do their own simplified graphic layouts. I would get jobs three times a week and the rest of the week, work on my paintings. I rarely had a social life due to the hours I would work. Sometimes, it would be 11-6, 3pm to 2am, 8pm- 4am. However the pay was more than a paste-up mechanical would make. With most of the money made, I managed to save and travel to third world nations to photograph how local people work and survive under worse working conditions. Unfortunately, Americans are not interested unless we are invading their territories.

After working as a fulltime employee at the American Museum of America. I encountered the "glass ceiling". My title was copy editor but I transferred raw copy to formatted text for Micropaleontology

Press. I worked there for 8 years until I mentioned "Save the children" for a misjudgment and I got booted out for being a "whistleblower". I used my vacation time to attend a woman's Buddhist conference in Leh, Ladakh, North India. There, I saw many women working hard in an agrarian feudal culture according to Buddha's text. Especially, if she wanted to be "spiritually" educated, she would have to work in the fields 6am-6pm and then in a poorly misshaped nunnery learn Buddhism text (reading & writing) until midnight.

One of my last jobs was working for the Brooklyn Daily Eagle that has a long historic background and I as a poet felt honored as well as privileged to work in a journalistic environment. However, due to sexual harassment I could not continue there if men are constantly lifting and unzipping their zippers in front of me.

——

Bio: *(Susan L. Yung)* **Domestic–violence; misogynist–hater; anti–racist; democractic–anarchist; ghettoe–girl; Chinatown–Harlem; East Village–West Village; homesteader–gentrifier; yuppie–squatter; homeless–sheltered; American–Asian; World–Traveller; Adventress–Common–Law–Wife; Photographer–Videographer; Martial–Fine–Artist; Musician–Drummer; Artist–Scientist; Geologist–Librarian; Mathematician–Designer; Collector–Exhibitionist; Buyer–Seller; Cook–Politician; Migrant–worker; Independent–Dependent; Pacifist–Activist.**

Girl Weaving Basket in Cebu, The Philippines to Sell in Bloomingdales, 1984

Nuns Sewing in Leh, Ladakh, India, 1995

•

ROGUE SCHOLARS
Press

For more information or a price quote
for our book design services, go to:

http://www.roguescholars.com

For General Information, e-mail:
info@roguescholars.com

Editor-In-Chief, C. D. Johnson:
editor-in-chief@roguescholars.com

•

Visit Us At:

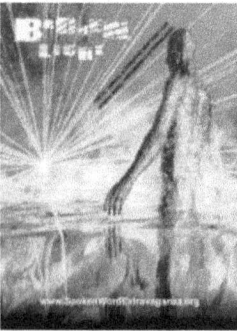  

  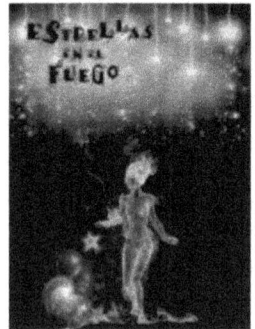

http://spokenwordextravaganza.org/

www.ingramcontent.com/pod-product-compliance
Lightning Source LLC
LaVergne TN
LVHW041155080426
835511LV00006B/611